The Great Experiment

This exhibition has been made possible through the generous support of

J. P. Morgan & Co. Incorporated

Mr. and Mrs. Charles T. Munger   Dr. and Mrs. Peter S. Bing

The National Endowment for the Humanities,

dedicated to expanding American understanding of

human experience and cultural heritage

The Gilder Lehrman Institute of American History

The Dan Murphy Foundation

Mr. and Mrs. Lloyd E. Cotsen

Mr. and Mrs. R. J. Munzer

Mr. and Mrs. H. Russell Smith

With special appreciation to the lenders to the exhibition

The Gilder Lehrman Collection

The Pierpont Morgan Library

The Mount Vernon Ladies' Association

The National Museum
of American History, Smithsonian Institution

The Louise and Barry Taper Collection

Dr. Gary Milan

The Great Experiment

George Washington
and the
American Republic

JOHN RHODEHAMEL

Foreword by Gordon S. Wood

Catalogue of an exhibition organized by
THE HUNTINGTON LIBRARY
with additional material from
THE GILDER LEHRMAN COLLECTION and
THE PIERPONT MORGAN LIBRARY

San Marino, California, The Huntington Library
October 1998–May 1999
New York City, The Pierpont Morgan Library
September–December 1999

Yale University Press   New Haven & London
The Huntington Library   San Marino, California

Designed by James J. Johnson and set in
Monotype Bulmer and Baskerville types by
Ink, Inc., New York.
Printed in the United States of America by
R. R. Donnelley & Sons, Roanoke, Virginia.

Library of Congress Catalog Card
Number 98-60559
ISBN 0-300-07614-2 (cloth: alk. paper)
ISBN 0-87328-174-8 (paper: alk. paper)

A catalogue record for this book is available
from the British Library.

The paper in this book meets the guidelines
for permanence and durability of the
Committee on Production Guidelines for Book
Longevity of the Council on Library
Resources.

10   9   8   7   6   5   4   3   2   1

Contents

Foreword

———◆◦◦◆———

THIS EXHIBITION commemorates the two-hundredth anniversary of George Washington's death. In a famous funeral oration in 1799, Henry Lee declared that Washington was the "first in war, first in peace, and first in the hearts of his country-men." This phrase has reverberated through the decades but with ever-weakening meaning. Many Americans today seem to have forgotten why Washington was truly a great man and our greatest president ever. We hope that this exhibition will help recall his greatness and explain not only why he fully deserved the accolades of his contemporaries but also why he ought to be first in the hearts of all Americans, even two centuries later.

No doubt Washington is not easy to understand. He quickly became, even in his own lifetime, more a monument than a man. Every passing year made him a less accessible human being. By the early decades of the nineteenth century he had already become statuesque and impenetrable. Through the years there have been periodic efforts to bring him down to earth, to expose his foibles, to debunk his fame, but he has remained massively monumental. Now, in the late twentieth century, he seems so far removed from us as to be virtually incomprehensible. He seems to come from another time and another place—from another world.

And that is the whole point about him: he does come from another world. Washington was the only truly classical hero we Americans have ever had. He belonged to the pre-democratic and pre-egalitarian world of the eighteenth century, to a world we have lost and that was being lost even as Washington lived.

In many respects Washington was an unlikely hero. To be sure, he had all the physical attributes of a classical hero. He was very tall by contemporary standards, and he was heavily built and a superb athlete. Physically he had what both men and women admired. He was both a splendid horseman at a time when that skill really counted and an extraordinarily graceful dancer, and naturally he loved both riding and dancing. He always moved with dignity and looked the leader.

Yet those who knew him well and talked with him were often disappointed. He never seemed to have much to say. He was most certainly not what one today would call an intellectual. Even Thomas Jefferson, who was unusually generous in his estimate of his friends, said that Washington's "colloquial talents were not above mediocrity." He had "neither copiousness of ideas nor fluency of words." Although Washington may not have been an intellectual, he was a man of affairs. He knew how to run his plantation and make it pay. He certainly ran Mount Vernon better than Jefferson ran Monticello. Washington's heart was always at Mount Vernon; he thought about it all the time. Even when Washington was president he devoted a great amount of energy to worrying about the fence posts on his plantation, and his letters dealing with the details of running Mount Vernon were longer than those dealing with the running of the federal government.

But being a man of affairs and running a plantation or even the federal government efficiently were not what made him a world-renowned hero. Neither were his military exploits. Washington was not a traditional military hero. He did not resemble Alexander, Caesar, Cromwell, or Marlborough; his military achievements were nothing compared with those that Napolean would soon have. Washington had no smashing, stunning victories. He was not a military genius, and his tactical and strategic maneuvers were not the sort that awed men. Military glory was not the source of his reputation. The real source of Washington's greatness lay in his moral character.

Washington was a man of virtue, but this virtue was not given to him by nature. He had to work for it, to cultivate it, and his contemporaries knew that he did. Washington was a self-made hero, and this impressed an eighteenth-century enlightened world that put great stock in men controlling both their passions and their destinies. Washington possessed a self-cultivated nobility. As his youthful copying of 110 maxims of civility from a courtesy book indicates, Washington was obsessed with behaving in a proper and dignified manner. This self-restraint dictated his behavior during the war—his willingness to defer to civilian leadership under trying conditions and, as his address to his officers in March 1783 indicates, his refusal to countenance any sort of military coup d'état against Congress. His most virtuous act, the one that made him famous, was his resignation in December 1783 as commander-in-chief of the American forces. This act, together with his June 1783 circular letter to the states in which he promised to retire forever from public life, was his legacy to his countrymen. No American leader has ever left a more important legacy.

His retirement at the height of his power was unprecedented in modern times. Cromwell, William of Orange, Marlborough—all had sought political rewards commensurate with their military achievements. Though it was widely thought that Washington could have become king or dictator, he wanted nothing of the kind. He was sincere in his desire for all the soldiers "to return to their Private Stations in the bosom of a free, peaceful and happy Country," and everyone recognized his sincerity. His retirement awed people on both sides of the Atlantic and made him an international hero.

Washington was not naive. He was well aware of the effect that his resignation would have. He was trying to live up to the age's image of a classical disinterested patriot who devotes his life to his country, and he knew at once that he had acquired fame as a modern Cincinnatus, the Roman who returned to his farm after saving his country. All of Washington's subsequent reluctance to exercise political power stemmed from the promise he had made in 1783.

Yet he was pressured by others to come out of retirement. His country needed him. The Philadelphia Convention could not have met in 1787 without him. The Constitution could not have been ratified in 1788 without his support. And the new federal government could not have been launched in 1789 without his being president. James Madison thought that Washington as president was the only part of the new government that captured the minds of the people. He filled out the executive, established its independence, and gave it the dignity many thought it needed. Even the scale and the grandeur of the capital city that came to bear his name owed much to his vision and his retention of Pierre L'Enfant as architect. If Jefferson had had his way, L'Enfant would never had kept this job as long as he did, and the capital would surely have been smaller and less magnificent.

As in the case of his career as commander-in-chief, his most important act as president was his giving up of the office. Most people assumed that Washington might be president as long as he lived, that he would be a kind of elective monarch. Hence his sincere desire to retire from the presidency enhanced his moral authority and helped fix the republican character of the Constitution. He was talked out of retiring in 1792, but in 1796 he was so determined to retire that no one could dissuade him. His leaving of office after two terms set a precedent that was not broken until Franklin D. Roosevelt secured a third term in 1940. His retirement was an object lesson in republicanism at a time when the republican experiment throughout the Atlantic world was very much in doubt.

Washington's final years in retirement were not happy ones. The American political world was changing, and Washington struggled to comprehend the changes. During his last years in office he and his Federalist administration had been subjected to vicious partisan criticism, and he felt the criticism deeply. By the end of the decade he had become increasingly disillusioned with the ways of American politics. In July 1799, Governor Jonathan Trumbull of Connecticut, with the backing of many Federalists, urged Washington once again to stand for the presidency in 1800. Only Washington, said Trumbull, could unite the Federalists and save the country from a "French President" backed by a radical Republican party. In his reply—one of the important documents displayed in the exhibition—Washington explained that new political conditions in the country made his candidacy irrelevant. In this new democratic era of party politics, he said, "personal influence," distinctions of character, no longer mattered. If the members of the Republican Party "set up a broomstick" as a candidate and called it a "true son of Liberty" or a "Democrat" or "any other epithet that will suit their purpose," it still would "command their votes in toto!" But even worse, the same was true of the Federalists. Party spirit now ruled, and people voted only along party lines. Even if he were the Federalist candidate, Washington was "thoroughly convinced I should not draw a single vote from the anti-federal side." Therefore his standing for election made no sense; he would "stand upon no stronger ground than any other Federal character well supported."

Washington wrote all this in anger and despair, and though he exaggerated, he was essentially right. The political world was changing, becoming democratic, and parties, not great men, would soon become the objects of contention. To be sure, Americans continued to long for great heroes as leaders, and right up through Eisenhower we have periodically elected Washingtons-manqué to the presidency. But democracy made such great heroes no longer essential to the workings of American government. And Washington, more than any other individual, was the one who made that kind of democratic government possible. As Jefferson said, "The moderation and virtue of a single character ...probably prevented this revolution from being closed, as most others have been, by a subversion of that liberty it was intended to establish."

Washington was an extraordinary man who made it possible for ordinary men to rule. There has been no president quite like him, and we can be sure that we shall not see his like again.

GORDON S. WOOD
Alva O. Way University Professor and Professor of History
Brown University

A Note from the Director

————◆❖◆————

HENRY HUNTINGTON was once asked why he declined to authorize a biography. "The Library will tell the story," he replied. The books scholars have published and the exhibitions the curatorial staff have mounted from the Library's resources, since its opening in 1924, have fulfilled Mr. Huntington's prediction. "The Great Experiment: George Washington and the American Republic" is the latest in a series of major exhibitions the Library has planned to inform the public about the history of America, based on documentary and artifactual evidence.

The Huntington's evidentiary approach to its exhibitions is particularly apt for George Washington, who today, 215 years into the American republic, is more a mythic or iconographical figure than a real person. John Rhodehamel's exhibition and catalogue serve to humanize Washington. One will not find here the apocryphal stories about chopping down the cherry tree or casting a silver dollar across the Potomac. Instead, the Huntington exhibition offers authentic evidence of Washington's integrity, physical prowess, and leadership through contemporary paintings, maps, objects, manuscripts, letters, and published writings.

In 1754, for example, at the age of twenty-one, Washington wrote and published in Williamsburg *The Journal of Major George Washington*, recounting his expedition into the Ohio Valley just before the Seven Years' War. In this early work, we see a young man, certainly courageous but not a little ambitious and self-serving.

Twenty-one years later, Washington, in accepting the position of general and leader of the Continental Army at the beginning of the Revolutionary War, is a man transformed. Weathering the Stamp Act and the Intolerable Acts along with his fellow colonists, he has come to realize that America, not England, is his country, and he put service to his country before his own ambitions. It is a transformation remarkable for its human scale.

Washington's later writings show him to be a man still imbued with courage but also reflective and in some cases doubtful. He demonstrates his integrity by resigning his commission and returning to farm Mount Vernon at the end of the war. Because of that integrity he is reluctant to return and stand for the presidency. In his finally accepting the position, he is mindful that there is no path before him: "I walk on untrodden ground," he said. "There is scarcely any part of my conduct which may not hereafter be drawn into precedent." In his first inaugural address, he notes that the "destiny of the Republican model of government [is] staked, on the experiment entrusted to the hands of the American people."

Our exhibition demonstrates both Washington's growth as a man and the untested government of the new United States of America. Older standard school texts take the new republic for granted, not recognizing the courage that it took for our fellow citizens of the eighteenth century to cut their ties from England and embark on their own way, with the cold North Atlantic separating them from the goods, services, and comforts of European civilization. Near the end of his life, Washington mused to Jefferson whether declaring independence and establishing the American republic would work. Washington died not knowing whether the great experiment was a success, but the example of his leadership has helped us since to make it so.

The Huntington Library could not have produced this exhibition, catalogue, and related educational programs without our partners and benefactors. Our thanks to the Pierpont

Morgan Library, where the exhibition will appear in the fall of 1999, and the Gilder Lehrman Collection for sharing materials from their collections. Many people and foundations provided the means for us to accomplish this exhibition: J. P. Morgan & Co. Incorporated; Mr. and Mrs. Charles T. Munger; Dr. and Mrs. Peter S. Bing; the National Endowment for the Humanities; the Gilder Lehrman Institute of American History; the Dan Murphy Foundation; Mr. and Mrs. Lloyd E. Cotsen; Mr. and Mrs. R. J. Munzer; Mr. and Mrs. H. Russell Smith. Our thanks to them all.

DAVID S. ZEIDBERG
R. Stanton & Ernestine Avery Director of the Library

Acknowledgments

———◆••◆———

THE HUNTINGTON LIBRARY gratefully acknowledges the contributions of the two institutions that joined with the Huntington to mount "The Great Experiment." At the Pierpont Morgan Library, we thank Charles Pierce and Robert Parks. At the Gilder Lehrman Collection, we are grateful for the support of Richard Gilder, Lewis E. Lehrman, James Basker, and Paul Romaine.

At Mount Vernon, we thank James Rees, John Riley, and James Kochan. At the Smithsonian Institution, thanks are due Harry Rubenstein. We are grateful for the expertise of the staff of Yale University Press, particularly Charles Grench and Heidi Downey.

The Huntington Library also recognizes the critical role played by the panel of distinguished American historians who served as scholarly consultants to the exhibition. They are W. W. Abbot of the University of Virginia, Joyce Appleby of the University of California at Los Angeles, Timothy Hall Breen of Northwestern University, Richard Lyman Bushman of Columbia University, Robert Middlekauff of the University of California at Berkeley, and Gordon S. Wood of Brown University.

Many Huntington staff members contributed to the exhibition. Within the Library Division they include, in the Department of Rare Books: Alan Jutzi, Lisa Libby, Maria Fredericks, Cathy Cherbosque, and Tom Canterbury; in the Department of Manuscripts: Mary Robertson, Dan Lewis, Lita Garcia, and Christine

Fagan; in Photographic Services: John Sullivan, Erin Wardlow, Grete Dalum-Tilds, Patricia Cornelius, Barbara Quinn, and Jan Pietrzak; in Preservation: Mark Roosa, Lauren Tawa, Susan Rogers, and Betsy Haude. Staff from other Huntington divisions also helped. They include Robert C. Ritchie, Peggy Park Bernal, Lee Devereux, and Carolyn Powell in the Research and Education Division; Marylyn Warren, Peggy Spear, and Catherine Babcock in the Development Division; Edward Nygren and Amy Meyers in the Art Division; and Anne Meyers and Laurie Sowd in the Financial Division.

The curator is more than grateful to his wife, Johanna Westerman Rhodehamel, whose idea for the title of the exhibition is among the least of the felicities she has bestowed upon him.

George Washington Chronology

—◆•◗◖•◆—

1732: Born February 22 near Popes Creek on Potomac River in Westmoreland County, Virginia.

1743: Father dies. Half brother Lawrence (born c. 1718) becomes GW's mentor.

1747: Copies out 110 "Rules of Civility." Studies mathematics and surveying. Formal education ends.

1748: Surveying trip to Shenandoah Valley provides first exposure to western frontier.

1749: Appointed surveyor of Culpeper County.

1750: Buys land in Shenandoah Valley.

1751: Sails to Barbados with Lawrence Washington, who seeks a cure for tuberculosis. Stricken with smallpox, GW gains lifelong immunity to the scourge of armies.

1752: Returns from Barbados. Lawrence Washington dies. Appointed major in Virginia militia.

1753: Carries British ultimatum demanding French withdrawal from Ohio Valley to French commandant at Fort Le Bouef near Lake Erie.

1754: Returns to Williamsburg with news of French defiance. Commissioned lieutenant colonel of militia. Defeats small enemy force, firing first shots of the Seven Years' War, or the French and Indian War. Surrenders to French after defeat at Fort Necessity.

1755: Survives Braddock's Defeat. Commissioned colonel commanding the Virginia Regiment.

1758: Commands two regiments in campaign that forces France from the Forks of the Ohio, ending war on Virginia's frontier. Resigns commission. Elected to Virginia Assembly.

1759: Marries Martha Dandridge Custis (b. 1731).

1767–73: Patents more than twenty thousand acres in western Virginia. Promotes plan to build canal and road system linking Potomac and Ohio rivers.

1774: Attends First Continental Congress in Philadelphia.

1775: Revolutionary War begins. Second Continental Congress names GW commander of new Continental Army. Assumes command at Cambridge, Massachusetts.

1776: British evacuate Boston. Opposing armies concentrate at New York. Defeated at battles of Long Island, Manhattan, and White Plains. Retreats through New Jersey and across Delaware River into Pennsylvania. Leads army back across river to defeat Hessian garrison at Trenton.

1777: Defeats small British force at Princeton. Defeated at battles of Brandywine and Germantown. Goes into winter quarters at Valley Forge, Pennsylvania.

1778: Treaty of alliance with France signed. Armies battle indecisively at Monmouth Court House.

1781: Commands American and French armies that force surrender of British army under Cornwallis at Yorktown, ending the military phase of the American Revolution.

1783: Britain formally recognizes American independence. Averts military coup d'état by dissatisfied officer corps at Newburgh, New York. Publishes farewell address, announcing intention to retire from public life forever and calling for "indissoluble Union of the States." Resigns commission. Returns to Mount Vernon.

1787: Serves as president of Philadelphia Convention that drafts United States Constitution.

1789: Elected president of the United States by unanimous vote in the Electoral College. Inaugurated in New York City. Appoints Alexander Hamilton secretary of the treasury, Henry Knox secretary of war, Thomas Jefferson secretary of state, and Edmund Randolph attorney general.

1792: Hopes to leave office when term ends in 1793. Persuaded to stay on, recognizing that the union cannot survive a contested presidential election. Reelected unanimously.

1793: Issues Proclamation of Neutrality when France declares war on Britain. Jefferson resigns.

1794: Dispatches John Jay to London as negotiator to avert war with Britain. Whiskey Rebellion collapses when GW leads twelve thousand troops into western Pennsylvania.

1795: Hamilton resigns. Jay's Treaty is attacked by opposition as pro-British, but GW wins struggle for its ratification.

1796: Publishes Farewell Address in Philadelphia newspaper.

1797: John Adams inaugurated president. GW returns to Mount Vernon.

1798: When war with France threatens, Adams appoints GW commander of New Army of the United States.

1799: Dismisses suggestions that he seek third presidential term in 1800. Dies at Mount Vernon on December 14.

The Great Experiment: Prologue

The establishment of our new Government seemed to be the
last great experiment for promoting human happiness.
—GEORGE WASHINGTON, January 9, 1790

GEORGE WASHINGTON took little interest
in his ancestors. In 1792, the president of the United
States replied politely to an English aristocrat who
had asked for help in tracing the Washington family
tree. Courtesy, however, did not disguise a pointed
little lecture on the promise of the great experiment then under
way. The Americans had set out to create a new society, one
guided by the faith that a person's rank should be grounded on
attainment rather than ancestry—by the faith that all were created equal.

His own ancestry was a subject, Washington wrote, "to
which I confess I have paid very little attention. My time has
been so much occupied in the busy and active scenes of life from
an early period of it that but a small portion of it could have
been devoted to researches of this nature.... We have no Office
of Record in this Country in which exact genealogical documents
are preserved; and very few cases, I believe, occur where a recur-
rence to pedigree for any considerable distance back has been
found necessary to establish such points as may frequently arise
in older Countries."

George Washington, autograph letter to Sir Isaac Heard, May 2, 1792.
(Huntington Library: HM 913)
Washington managed to include a lesson in republican principles in this letter to an aristocratic English genealogist.

Washington's veiled text might read: In republican society, people, though born equal, still seek the honors supplied by titles of nobility. A kind of loose republican aristocracy may exist in America, but entry into its ranks does not require fortunate birth, but rather demonstrated talent, ambition, and virtuous devotion to the public good. Washington had been too busy winning honor to study his lineage.

So much honor did he win that His Excellency General George Washington may seem an unlikely champion of the revolutionary principle that all people are created equal. Americans have revered Washington as a mythic figure, remote in his icy majesty. We cannot forget that he was the master of three hundred slaves. He was commander of officers and men in the thousands— the generalissimo awarded dictatorial powers by the Continental Congress in 1776. He was the consummate political actor who became America's first elected head of state. Washington was also a high-living Virginia gentleman who possessed vast tracts of land and all the luxuries wealth could command. He was an authentic classical hero—"the American Cincinnatus"—said to have had countless admirers but not a single friend. He was a proud but insecure man who could confuse dissent with disloyalty.

Yet this same George Washington was a revolutionary, for a quarter-century the central figure in a radical revolution that aimed at nothing less than the transformation of western civilization. When Washington was born in 1732, the British colonies in North America were obscure and inconsequential outposts. The courts of Europe had long been the focus of the Atlantic world. All the principal European states were ruled by hereditary monarchs—kings and queens, emperors and czars—who reigned by virtue of their carefully recorded pedigrees. In Britain the king was constrained by a constitution that compelled him to govern with the consent of Parliament, but even there the king was the unquestioned head of state. Just beneath royalty revolved the glittering constellations of aristocracy—noble peers, proud lords, and highborn ladies. They too were exalted by birth far above the common run of men and women. Government by birth appeared the most satisfactory model for ordering society, one that had prevailed for centuries and promised to persist into the remote future.

When Washington died in 1799, the age of hereditary power —the very notion of government by birth—was heading toward extinction. And the United States of America, overleaping its small beginnings on the margins of European civilization, was poised to thrust itself into the forefront of world history. The little republic was soon to become a gigantic continental democracy.

Although the promise of equality has never been completely fulfilled, the American Revolution made the theory of republican popular government a reality, furnishing a compelling alternative to the ancient tyranny of kings. American success marked a fundamental turning point in human affairs.

That success may have been out of reach without Washington's leadership. Of course George Washington did not make the Revolution; it was the work of the American people. The man who described himself as a "figure upon the stage" in the "Great Drama" "now acting in this theater" emerged as a flawless performer taking his cues from his audience—the people themselves. Although many Americans were shut out of the political process, participation by white men was widespread. They could draw on traditions extending back to the antique republics of Greece and Rome. Many had studied the political theorists of the Enlightenment. They could take pride in the venerable constitution of Britain itself, the set of customs that, Britons and their British-American cousins boasted, made England the most free nation on earth. The Americans also drew on their unique heritage as inhabitants of fluid, quasi-republican colonial societies.

Still, George Washington played the leading role at every stage of the drama of revolution and nation-building. Thomas Jefferson supposed that Washington's "was the singular destiny and merit, of leading the armies of his country successfully through an arduous war for the establishment of its independence; of conducting its councils through the birth of a government, new in forms and principles, until it settled down into a quiet and orderly train; and of scrupulously obeying the laws through the whole of his career, civil and military, of which the history of the world furnishes no other example."

Revolution is a perilous enterprise. You have a republic, but only if you can keep it, Benjamin Franklin had warned after the delegates signed the new Constitution. Would it prove, as philosophers predicted and as history seemed to confirm, that the republican government demanded by the principle of equality could never provide the bonds of power needed to hold together a large nation? Was it inevitable that, in a few years or decades, the United States would be forced to abandon popular elections and resort to despotism? Would the infant republic fragment into squabbling petty sovereignties?

We know the outcome of the experiment; those living through its early years could not. But they did understand what was at risk. They were contending for what Washington called the "destiny of unborn Millions." No one felt the gamble more keenly than he did. "The sacred fire of liberty, and the destiny of the Republican model of Government are…staked, on the experiment entrusted to the hands of the American people," he predicted at his first inauguration in 1789. Years after the older man's death Jefferson remembered that Washington had "often declared to me that he considered our new constitution as an experiment on the practicability of republican government, and with what dose of liberty man could be trusted for his own good; that he was determined the experiment should have a fair trial, and would lose the last drop of his blood in support of it."

It was not Washington's blood, however, but his enormous prestige, the trust that Americans held for him, that had carried the experiment through so many hazards. He had won that trust in the Revolution. He had won it by the extraordinary act of resigning his command at the end of the war. General Washington had led the American states to independent nationhood through eight years of war and diplomacy. But history had seen many victorious generals—many Caesars and Cromwells. What set this general apart was that he willingly, even eagerly, gave up power to return to Mount Vernon as a private citizen in 1783. This single act impressed the entire western world, as Washington had surely known it would. On both sides of the Atlantic, George Washington was regarded as the greatest man alive: the incorruptible republican hero. In an age that believed power inevitably corrupted its possessors, Washington was a wonder of the age.

Revolutions have a way of going bad—tyrants are often supplanted by greater tyrants. The greatest revolution of the eighteenth century broke out in Paris in 1789, the year that Washington became president. Fifteen years later the French Revolution succeeded in replacing a king with an emperor when Napoleon Bonaparte crowned himself in 1804. In America the outcome had been different. Jefferson concluded that the "moderation & virtue of a single character has probably prevented this revolution from being closed as most others have been, by a subversion of that liberty it was intended to establish."

Washington called this revolution the "last great experiment, for promoting human happiness." Throughout his life, however, he had been engaged in another experiment: while still a boy, he had begun a process of self-invention. On the success of the first endeavor would hinge the success of the other. The result of the personal experiment was Washington's deliberate creation of the monumental character that gave him the moral authority to lead the quarrelsome collection of little states into sturdy nationhood.

The American people themselves contributed to the creation of the monument. In 1776, riotous New Yorkers toppled the equestrian statue of His Britannic Majesty, King George III, from its pedestal in a Manhattan public square. (The leaden likeness was soon melted down for musket balls to fire at His Majesty's soldiery.) In 1792, citizens of the United States placed a statue of their first president on the same pedestal. The Americans had cast aside the pomp and heraldry of monarchical England. As they began to gather about their new republic the symbols of nationhood, they chose instead certain noble words, an eagle, a flag, and George Washington. "God save great Washington," they sang. "God damn the king."

The myth making began with Washington's appointment as commander of the Continental Army in 1775, and it continued long after his death. His identification with the new nation was so complete, and his heroic reputation so carefully contrived, that it is unlikely that the "real" Washington will ever escape the obscuring embrace of his mythological image. As one historian has astutely observed, "We may suspect, however, that myth and man can never be entirely separated, and that valuable clues to Washington's temperament, as well as his public stature, lie in this fact."

But George Washington did not get his start in life as a marble colossus on a pedestal. Washington's act of self-creation was one of the most comprehensive in all of America's long procession of self-made men.

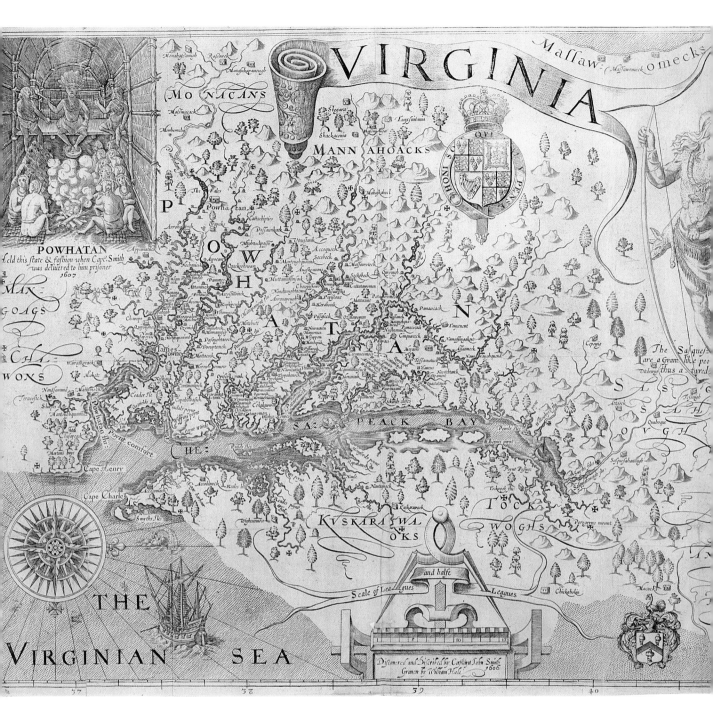

"Virginia Discovered and Discribed by Captain John Smith," in John Smith, *A Map of Virginia,* Oxford, 1612.

(Pierpont Morgan Library: PML 15911)

The English founded the colony of Virginia in 1607, fifty years before George Washington's great-grandfather sailed up the Potomac. The map is arranged with west at the top. Chesapeake Bay sprawls sideways across the chart, and the Potomac is the big river at the center.

Powerful Ambitions,
Powerful Friends

———— ◆•◆•◆ ————

ASHINGTON'S KNOWLEDGE of his forebears extended back only as far as his first American ancestor, his great-grandfather. "In the year 1657, or thereabouts," Washington wrote, "and during the Usurpation of Oliver Cromwell John and Lawrence Washington, Brothers Emigrated from the north of England, and settled at Bridges Creek, on Potomac river, in the County of Westmoreland." In that year the little *Sea Horse of London* had ascended Chesapeake Bay and sailed into the ten-mile-wide mouth of the Potomac. Along the distant shores stretched a landscape that dwarfed Europe in scale and richness.

This was the first American voyage of the mate, John Washington, a young man of good family whose prospects in England had been darkened by the Puritan revolution. In setting out on the return voyage, the tobacco-laden ketch ran upon a Potomac shoal and split her seams. The sailors went ashore. The mate must have liked what he saw there, for when the crew refloated *Sea Horse* and set sail for the Chesapeake Capes, Washington remained in

Virginia. He soon married the daughter of a prosperous planter and entered enthusiastically into the cycle of land, tobacco, and local politics, displaying the acquisitive drive that elevated men in the fifty-year-old colony. By the time of his death twenty years later the man who had come ashore empty-handed could claim more than five thousand acres, much of it laid out in tobacco plantations. His sons and grandsons followed a like pattern—marrying well; gathering in land, slaves, and county offices; growing tobacco; and dying in middle age.

John Washington's grandson Augustine died in 1743, a year

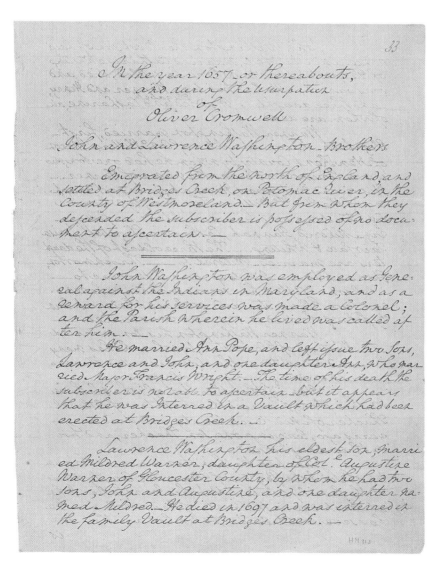

George Washington, autograph manuscript ("In the year 1657, or thereabouts"), May 2, 1792.

(Huntington Library: HM 913)
Three generations of the family had lived in Virginia before George Washington's birth. His family history opens with the arrival of his great-grandfather, John Washington: "In the year 1657—or thereabouts...John and Lawrence Washington— Brothers Emigrated from the north of England, and settled at Bridges Creek, on Potomac River." George Washington was born at Bridges Creek seventy-five years after the immigrant's arrival.

A Map of the Inhabited part of Virginia, . . . Drawn by Joshua Fry & Peter Jefferson in 1751, **London, 1755. Detail.**

(Huntington Library: 480575)

The Jefferson and Fry map's cartouche offered an emblem for the world into which George Washington was born in 1732. The Virginia colony was dominated by wealthy planters. Their status rested on the ownership of land, the labor of slaves, and the cultivation of tobacco. The younger son of a moderately prosperous planter, Washington, though a gentleman by birth, ranked with the lesser gentry.

short of his fiftieth birthday. He left behind a widow, Mary Ball Washington, and seven children, the two oldest from a previous marriage. The first-born of the children of the second marriage was George, born on February 22, 1732, in a four-room farmhouse set on the point where Popes Creek emptied into the broad Potomac. The estate amounted to ten thousand acres and fifty slaves. It was a respectable holding but hardly conspicuous in a colony where great families like the Byrds and Carters numbered their slaves in the hundreds and their acres in the many tens of thousands.

At best, George Washington had been born into the lower ranks of Virginia gentry. And, as a younger son by a second marriage, he was due at age twenty-one only a modest portion of his father's property—just a few hundred unpromising acres and ten slaves. The legacy of slavery would attend Washington all his life. There were likely slaves in the room where he was born; other slaves stood by quietly as he died sixty-seven years later. John

Washington had relied mostly on white indentured servants to work his tobacco fields. But in the half-century between the emigrant's death and the birth of his great-grandson, the Virginia colony had been transformed by the importation of tens of thousands of slaves from West Africa. By the time George Washington's childhood ended, Virginia's population approached a quarter-million, and as many as half were black slaves. Conditions of servitude were harsh. Coerced labor would allow men of the revolutionary generation to live well and devote their energies to the pursuit of honor through public service. But the enslavement of these new Americans from Africa was a tragedy that would haunt all Americans.

The death of Augustine Washington had far-reaching consequences. George's father and his half brothers had gone to school in England; his expectations of following them were now dashed. His inheritance was probably too meager to establish him as an independent planter. George Washington would have to make his own way in the world. The boy had spent his earliest years at Popes Creek, at Ferry Farm near the Rappahannock river town of Fredericksburg, and at a new plantation on the upper Potomac. Here Augustine Washington had built a house on a high bluff commanding spectacular views of the big river and the wooded Maryland shore. After his father's death George found himself at Ferry Farm with his mother and his younger siblings.

Fortunately, he was not lacking a figure on which to model himself. His half-brother Lawrence, fourteen years his senior, must have been the glorious embodiment of everything George hoped to be. Lawrence was an English-educated gentleman who had married into northern Virginia's most powerful family, the Fairfaxes. He was able and highly ambitious, and as eldest son he had inherited the bulk of Augustine Washington's estate. Lawrence was adjutant general of the colony's militia and had been elected to the House of Burgesses, Virginia's legislative assembly.

Lawrence Washington must have seen promise in his little brother, for he set out to train him for success, starting him on the road he so eagerly followed to wealth, fame, and power. Lawrence Washington was the most important influence on George Washington's life.

In 1740, Lawrence had served as a Virginia officer in the disastrous British siege of Spanish Cartagena. Most of the Virginia troops died, and the lucky survivors were left with bitter memories of mistreatment at the hands of supercilious British regulars. Still, Major Washington came away from the experience with enough admiration for his commander, Admiral Edward Vernon, to name his plantation Mount Vernon in his honor. Here Lawrence and his bride lived in his father's house, with its sweeping Potomac vistas. His wife was the former Anne Fairfax, daughter of William Fairfax, who was himself the cousin and Virginia agent of the great Thomas, sixth Baron Fairfax of Cameron. Lord Fairfax, on the strength of his fortunate birth and a dead king's gift, was proprietor of the vast Northern Neck of Virginia. The Fairfax Proprietary took in all the land between the Potomac and Rappahannock rivers, a staggering five million acres.

Whenever he could escape his mother's grasp, George Washington now passed his time at Mount Vernon, where he was drawn into the aristocratic orbit of the powerful Fairfax family. The alliance was to be of the utmost importance in his progress as a gentleman, soldier, politician, and landholder.

Washington's formal education ended when he was about fifteen. Since he was not destined for the privileged life of a gentleman planter, his were not the opportunities accorded to the more fortunate Virginians of the time. He did not go to school in England like his older brothers. He did not attend Virginia's College of William and Mary or a northern university, as did such men as Thomas Jefferson and James Madison. His education seems to have been largely practical, as befitted one who was soon to be earning a living.

Surviving copybooks reveal that he studied mathematics, surveying, and geography, along with the legal forms and accounting

methods used in plantation business. He learned to write in an elegant, flowing hand. He also mastered the English language itself. The man who would compose thousands of documents probably taught himself to write by emulating the prose he read. He would become a forceful writer, capable at times of passages of compelling eloquence. Reading also helped Washington to absorb the code of conduct that was as essential to his advancement as his native drive and talent.

Most famous of his bids to gain a gentleman's polish was his exercise, at age fifteen, of copying the 110 "Rules of Civility and Decent Behaviour in Company and Conversation," a collection of maxims compiled in 1595. The rules gently instruct those most in need of advice not to undress in public and to "bedew no mans face with your Spittle." But more advanced students could acquire a good grounding in the diplomatic skills that a beginner needed to get ahead—those ceremonies of deference due the powerful, the kind of behavior that won a man respect for himself.

It was the Fairfax association that gave Washington his introduction to the western frontier, where an approaching war was soon to bring him fame at an early age. Two weeks past his sixteenth birthday he joined a month-long expedition to survey some of his lordship's frontier lands in the Shenandoah Valley. The journey was a revelation to the young man. Here, little more than a day's ride from the scenes of his boyhood, was a fresh country of almost unimaginable richness. The vision of a spacious western destiny would absorb Washington until the day he died. The promise of the west would shape his judgment as a soldier, land speculator, and canal builder, and later as a statesman and an advocate of American union. That these dreams of empire

Stem from a calumet.
(National Museum of American History, Smithsonian Institution: 67435, 31822)
Sixteen-year-old George Washington shared this peace pipe with an Indian chief during his first journey to the western frontier in 1748.

demanded the violent dispossession of the region's native peoples was a grim concomitant that apparently never gave Washington much regret.

Washington knew that some western lands could be secured on attractive terms from those fortunate enough to possess the patronage of Lord Fairfax. In 1747 the eccentric peer had crossed the ocean and taken up residence in his forest domain. Before long, George Washington was ushered into the great man's presence. The nobleman encountered a striking youth. The earliest description, though written a decade later, yields a glimpse of the younger Washington. He was as

> straight as an Indian, measuring 6 feet 2 inches in his stockings, and weighing 175 pounds.... His frame is padded with well developed muscles, indicating great strength. His bones and joints are large as are his hands and feet. He is wide shouldered.... His head is well shaped, though not large, but is gracefully poised on a superb neck. A large and straight rather than a prominent nose; blue-grey penetrating eyes which are widely separated and overhung by a heavy brow. A pleasing and benevolent tho a commanding countenance.... In conversation he looks you full in the face, is deliberate, deferential, and engaging. His demeanor at all times composed and dignified. His movements and gestures are graceful, his walk majestic, and he is a splendid horseman.

For the next fifty years observers would stress the same qualities—Washington's great strength, his majestic bearing (his height was actually 6 feet 3), the reserve with which he set himself apart from others, and his air of command. A head taller than most men of his time, he seemed to have been born to lead them. But his most significant trait was not so apparent to the eye: the young Washington was consumed by ambition. Understanding this fierce ambition, and how he would harness it for the service of a cause greater than that of his own advancement, is the key to penetrating Washington's abiding mystery.

Pursuant to a Warrant from the Proprietors Office to Me directed I have Survey'd for Andrew Viney Three hundred and Eighty Six Acres and a Quarter of Waste and Ungranted Land Situate in Augusta County and on the Lost River or Cacapehon &c Bounded as followeth

Beginning at a Large white Pine and three Lynn Trees growing from one stump and on the East side the River and run thence No 55 Wt Three hundred Poles to three white Oaks amongst the Ridges of the Mountaine thence So 35 Et Two hundred and Six Poles to a white Oak Black Oak and Hickory thence So 55 Et Three hundd Poles to a Maple Lynn and wild Cherry Trees on the Mountain side not far from the River thence No 35 Et Two hundred and Six poles to the Beginning this Eighth Day of November 1749

by GW
Washington SCC

John Lonem
Edward Corder } Cha: Men

Andrew Viney Marker

George Washington, autograph survey, November 8, 1749.

(Pierpont Morgan Library: MA 3461)

Washington started out in life as a surveyor in the Shenandoah Valley. He was just seventeen when he executed this handsome plat. Frontier life strengthened the massive young man and gave him a knowledge of the forests that few Virginians of the gentry class could claim.

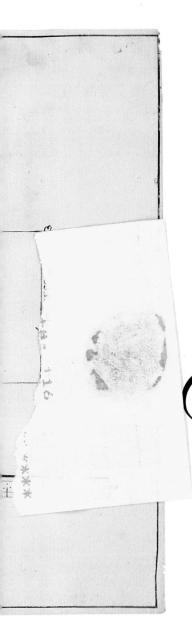

War for North America

*I*N 1754 LIEUTENANT COLONEL George Washington of the Virginia Regiment fired the first shots of one of history's great wars, a global conflict that decided the future of a continent and set the stage for the American Revolution.

His path to that bloody skirmish in the Pennsylvania forest had begun within the walls of Belvoir, the fashionable Fairfax mansion near Mount Vernon. In 1749, his Fairfax connection had gained for Washington the lucrative post of surveyor of Culpeper County, a new frontier district carved out of the Northern Neck Proprietary. A woodsman's life further hardened the tough young man, and here he lay the foundations of his fortune, clearing as much as £150 a year. By 1750 he was able to buy his first tract of land. But visions of far greater wealth beckoned from beyond the western horizon, across the mountains that hemmed in the Shenandoah Valley. A group of influential Anglo-Virginians had secured King George II's grant to hundreds of thousands of acres in the Ohio country. Ohio Company partners included Lawrence

Washington and Lieutenant Governor Robert Dinwiddie, the highest-ranking English official in Virginia. The company sent out explorers and began to blaze a road.

The Ohio Valley, however, was not a "wilderness" but a land inhabited for centuries by tribes determined to resist the newcomers' invasion. Of more immediate concern to the Virginians were the imperial pretensions of France, Britain's ancient European rival. The French held Canada and the lower Mississippi and also had a claim to the Ohio. When word reached Virginia that the French soldiers were building forts in the region, it seemed that the Ohio Company's enterprise might soon dissolve. With the governor and key members of the colonial assembly deeply involved in the scheme, Virginia's official western policy and the private interests of its leaders were knitted into an unseemly tangle. Much alarmed, Governor Dinwiddie appealed to his superiors, reminding London that Virginia had long claimed the beaches of the Pacific as its western border: France had insolently invaded English soil.

In October 1753, King George II's royal command reached Williamsburg. Dinwiddie was to require any "Europeans not our subjects" "peaceably to depart" from the Ohio. Should they refuse, the Virginians must "drive them out by force of arms." To reach the French, however, the king's ultimatum had to be conveyed in the dead of winter across hundreds of miles of rugged country, across unmapped mountains and forests ruled by hostile or unpredictable warriors. Still, one eager young Virginian saw his great opportunity approaching in this long-awaited collision of empires.

George Washington had lost his patron when Lawrence died in 1752, probably of tuberculosis, at thirty-four. But the loss did not deflect him from his ambitious course. Lawrence had headed the Virginia militia, and soon after his death, Washington, although he could claim no military experience whatsoever, was campaigning for his brother's place. The post was eventually divided into four independent commands, and one of them, carrying the rank of major and a £100 salary, went to George Wash-

ington, aged twenty. When he heard of the pending mission to the west, Major Washington hurried to Williamsburg to volunteer as diplomatic courier. Dinwiddie accepted.

Washington would later remember that "it was deemed by some an extraordinary circumstance that so young and inexperienced a person should have been employed on a negotiation with which subjects of the greatest importance were involved." But Dinwiddie's choice was not so strange. No crude pioneer or Indian trader would do to carry the king's message to the French commandant. Major Washington was a gentleman. Perhaps no Virginian of equal social standing had as much personal knowledge of the frontier.

Washington also looked as though he might survive the dangerous mission. He would have to handle Britain's Iroquois allies diplomatically. He would have to deal even more gingerly with the "French Indians" who had "taken up the Hatchet against the English." As he would soon demonstrate, this young man was almost entirely without fear. An artist who looked into Washington's eyes and captured their piercing challenge on canvas was convinced that "had he been born in the forests he would have been the fiercest man among the savage tribes." Dinwiddie surely detected the iron in the major's backbone, just as he must have sensed his intelligence and ambition.

Washington started west with a small party of frontiersmen. A month of hard marching and tricky negotiations with the Iroquois was required to reach Venago, a little fort that flew the flag of France. The officers within received Washington cordially but told him that they had no authority to treat with an ambassador. They sent him on to their commander at a more distant fort, though not before favoring him with the intelligence that "it was their absolute Design to take Possession of the Ohio, & by G— they would do it."

It was the middle of December before Washington could present the British ultimatum to the French commandant near

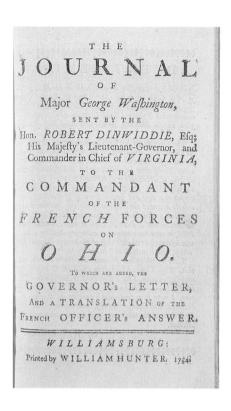

George Washington, *The Journal of Major George Washington, Sent...to the Commandant of the French Forces on the Ohio.* Williamsburg, 1754.

(Huntington Library: 18718)

Washington's account of this dangerous mission brought him fame on both sides of the Atlantic. Major Washington had fought his way across hundreds of miles of frozen wilderness to deliver the British ultimatum demanding French withdrawal from the contested Ohio Valley. When the French refused to give up their claim to the Ohio, war was inevitable. The Huntington Library's copy of the Williamsburg edition of *The Journal* is one of eight known to survive.

the shores of Lake Erie. Washington was surely not surprised when that aristocratic officer politely informed him that France was not obliged to obey the dictates of the English king. French defiance meant war, and that news must reach Williamsburg as soon as possible. The journey home was a nightmarish ordeal. The horses gave out. Washington's woodsmen could not keep up with him. With a single guide he fought on through thigh-deep snow and subfreezing temperatures. The two men almost died when a mysterious Indian fired on them from close range. Washington nearly perished again when he fell from a raft into the ice-choked Allegheny River.

He reached Williamsburg on January 16, 1754. Governor Dinwiddie wanted a written report at once. Washington probably got little rest during the day and night he spent composing the seven-thousand-word account. Dinwiddie rushed it into print as *The Journal of Major George Washington, Sent...to the Commandant of the French Forces on the Ohio.* Reprinted in London and the colonies, the little

"Map of the Western parts of the Colony of Virginia, as far as the Mississipi," in George Washington, *The Journal of Major George Washington...,* London, 1754.

(Gilder Lehrman Collection, on deposit at the Pierpont Morgan Library: GLC00419)

The collision of French and British imperial ambitions in the Ohio Valley ignited the

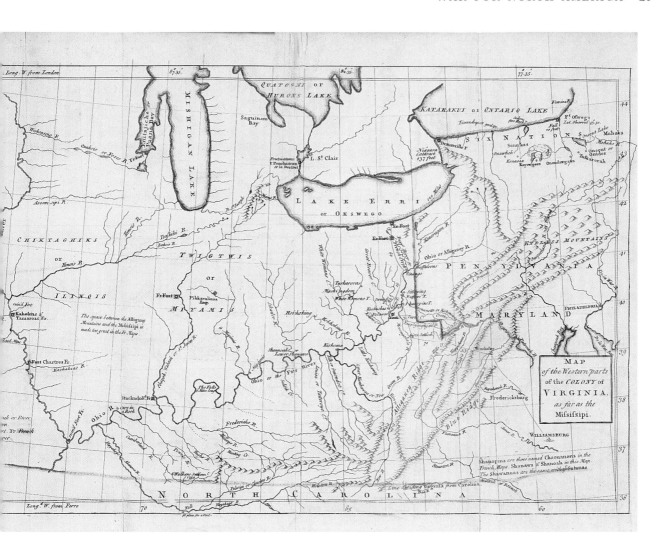

global conflict known as the Seven Years' (or French and Indian) War. Washington's soldiers fired the first shots of that great war in a little skirmish in May 1754. This map from the London edition of Major Washington's *Journal* shows the vast region for which the two European powers fought.

book made Washington's name known on both sides of the Atlantic, an uncommon distinction for any American. The perilous mission had yielded shining success. Major Washington was soon promoted to lieutenant colonel, second in command of the Virginia Regiment. He had just turned twenty-two.

The key to the region that Washington had traversed was the Forks of the Ohio, where the Allegheny and Monongahela formed the Ohio River. A fort on the point where the swift waters rushed together would control those waterways, and thus the Ohio Valley. By the time the snows had melted from the mountainsides, Washington was headed west with a detachment of one hundred sixty volunteers and orders to occupy the Forks. He soon learned that more than a thousand French soldiers had already seized the confluence, where they were building the stronghold they called Fort Duquesne. Nevertheless, Washington elected to push ahead. On May 28, 1754, he surprised a small party of French soldiers encamped in the woods near Great Meadows. About ten of the enemy, including their commander, fell to bullets or Iroquois hatchets. The captured survivors insisted that theirs had been a peaceful diplomatic mission, like Washington's a few months earlier, to deliver an ultimatum demanding British withdrawal from territory claimed by France. Though he maintained that the French officer had been a spy, Washington stood accused of murdering an ambassador.

News of the tiny battle electrified Europe. From opposite sides of the Channel, French and English observers alike would marvel that a few shots fired by an obscure soldier in the backwoods of America had struck a spark that "set the world ablaze." That blaze was to consume more than one million lives in battles fought around the globe. War was already inevitable, and although it was not formally declared until 1756, the great struggle commenced at the moment Washington attacked the luckless Frenchmen. The Seven Years' War—known as the French and Indian War in America—would involve not only Britain and France and their colonies, but also Austria, Prussia, Russia, Spain, Portugal, and most of the German states.

Washington's letter to a brother—in which he bragged that "I heard Bulletts whistle and believe me there was something charming in the sound"—was published in the London press. On reading it, King George II sniffed, "He would not say so, if he had been used to hear many." It would not be the last time that George Washington would attract the attention of a British monarch. But Great Meadows was his last victory for some time to come.

Washington was now a full colonel commanding the regiment. He built a fort on exposed low ground about fifty miles from the Forks. At Fort Necessity he and his men awaited certain attack by a superior enemy. His blunders were rewarded with a siege that came in a downpour that drenched the defenders' gunpowder. From the hills around the badly sited fort enemy marksmen kept up a steady fire that cut down a third of Washington's officers and men. The Virginians surrendered on July 7. The victors permitted the garrison to march out with their weapons and return to Virginia unmolested. They did require, however, that Washington sign a surrender document written in French. Since the young officer could read no language but English, he may not have known that the paper contained his admission that he had "assassinated" the French ambassador at Great Meadows.

Despite the disaster at Fort Necessity, George Washington remained a hero to many. Few Virginians seemed to notice that their frontier warrior had probably exceeded his orders and had certainly demonstrated considerable incompetence as a strategist. But others understood how badly he had blundered. Washington had been ordered to fight only if the French provoked attack. War may have been inevitable, but it would have been wise to delay its outbreak. His impetuous behavior had dismayed and estranged the tribes allied with Britain, and the ambassador's death gave France a welcome propaganda victory. The success of the journey to the French commandant was eclipsed by the hollow victory and the humiliating defeat that followed. In Europe, Washington would soon be mocked as a bumbling provincial or denounced as an unprincipled assassin. It must have been with some trepidation that the colonel next entered Governor Dinwiddie's office.

His fears were realized a few months later, when the governor announced his decision to divide the Virginia Regiment into companies. Captain would be the highest rank that any serving officer could hold. Rather than accept such a demotion, Colonel Washington angrily resigned his commission. (Rank had long been a galling issue for the Virginian. He had been infuriated to learn

GEORGE R.

WHEREAS fome Doubts have arifen with regard to the Rank and Command, which Officers and Troops raifed by the Governors of Our Provinces in *North-America*, fhould have, when joined, or ferving together with Our Independent Companies of Foot, doing Duty in our faid Provinces. In order to fix the fame, and to prevent for the future all Difputes on that Account, We are hereby pleafed to declare, that it is Our Will and Pleafure that all Troops ferving by Commiffion figned by Us, or by Our General commanding in Chief

(2)

Chief in *North-America* ; fhall take Rank before all Troops, which may ferve by Commiffion from any of the Governors, Lieutenant or Deputy - Governors, or Prefident, for the Time being, of Our Provinces in *North-America* : And it is Our farther Pleafure, that the General and Field-Officers of the Provincial-Troops, fhall have no Rank with the General and Field-Officers, who ferve by Commiffion from Us ; But that all Captains, and other inferior Officers of Our Forces, who are, or may be employ'd, in *North America*, are on all Detachments, Courts-Martial, or other Duty, wherein They may be joined with Officers, ferving by Commiffion from the Governors, Lieutenant or Deputy - Governors, or Prefident for the Time being of the faid Provinces, to command and take Poft of the faid Provincial Officers of the like Rank, though the Commiffions of the faid

George II, *Orders for Settling the Rank of the Officers of HM's Forces, When Serving with the Provincial Forces in North America*, London, 1754.

(Huntington Library: 71480)
The British regarded American soldiers, even ranking officers like Washington, with disdain. This royal decree of King George II ruled that regular British officers outranked any American commander. George Washington never forgave the British Empire for the insult.

that English officers holding a regular army commission outranked any colonial militia officer, even a colonel commanding a regiment. All his attempts to secure a regular commission had been unavailing.)

Meanwhile, the British government had dispatched a formidable expeditionary force—two crack regiments commanded by Major General Edward Braddock, the haughty veteran of many a European battlefield. The powerful army was to start west from Virginia in the spring of 1755. Washington perceived a new opportunity and offered his services to the general. Braddock was happy to add the young Virginian, who had actually seen the disputed Forks and fought the enemy, to his personal staff.

Although Braddock esteemed Washington, he had little but contempt for colonial soldiers. He believed that American militiamen were military incompetents, and most of them cowards to boot. Braddock's contempt for the enemy was deeper still. The "*regularity* and *discipline*" that had so often prevailed in Europe—massed lines of infantry exchanging volleys before the vaunted

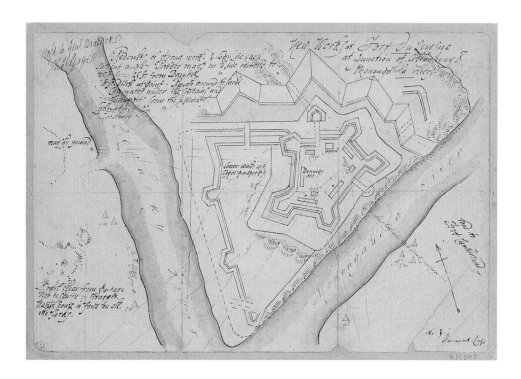

"New Works at Fort du Quesne at junction of Alligheny & Monougahila rivers," manuscript map, 1755.

(Huntington Library: HM 898) General Edward Braddock's own map of Fort Duquesne is a relic of Braddock's Defeat. On July 9, 1755, Braddock's powerful army was destroyed by French and Indian fighters just outside the fort. This map was found in the general's military chest by the victorious French after the battle. The most celebrated survivor of the slaughter was George Washington, who displayed courage that won him acclaim in Britain and America.

redcoats unleashed their irresistible bayonet charge—would certainly triumph over any foe encountered in the wilds of America.

By midsummer, Braddock's two thousand regulars and five hundred colonials were nearing the Forks of the Ohio. The general divided his force, leading a fast column of fifteen hundred ahead to attack Fort Duquesne. Though not yet recovered from a violent illness that had laid him low for weeks, barely able to mount a horse, Washington insisted on being in at the kill. He rode forward in pain to witness the capture of Fort Duquesne. Instead, he witnessed Braddock's Defeat, one of the most shocking episodes in British military history.

On July 9, 1755, just a few miles from the fort, several hundred French soldiers and native American warriors attacked and utterly routed the redcoats. It was just the sort of fatal trap that Washington had warned Braddock against. Most of the soldiers and almost every officer Braddock commanded that day were killed or wounded. The general himself fell with the bullet

To The Right Honourable, John, Earl of Loudon

General and Commander in Chief of all His
Majesty's Forces in North America and
Governor and Commander in Chief of His Majesty's
Most antient Colony and Dominion of Virginia

We the Officers of the Virginia Regiment beg Leave to congratulate Your
Lordship on your safe Arrival in America; And to express the deep Sense We have of
His Majesty's great Wisdom and paternal Care for his Colonies in sending your Lordship to
their Protection at this critical Juncture. We likewise beg Leave to declare our Singular
Satisfaction and sanguine Hopes on your Lordship's immediate Appointment over our
Colony, as it in a more especial Manner entitles Us to your Lordship's Patronage.

Full of Hopes that a perfect Union of the Colonies will be brought about by your
Lordship's Wisdom and Authority, and big with Expectations of seeing the extravagant Insolence
of an Insulting, Subtle and Inhuman Enemy restrained, and of having it in our
Power to take our desired Revenge: We humbly represent to your Lordship, that We were the
first Troops in Action on the Continent on Occasion of the present Broils, And that by
several Engagements and continual Skirmishes with the Enemy, We have to our Cost acquired
a Knowledge of Them, and of their crafty and cruel Practices, which We are ready to testify,
with the greatest Chearfulness and Resolution whenever We are so happy as to be honoured
with the Execution of your Lordship's Commands. —

In Behalf of the Corps

Winchester in Virginia
July 25th 1756

G. Washington, Col.

through his lungs that would kill him a few days later. George Washington heard the bullets whistle again. Indeed, four of them tore his coat, one carried off his hat, and two horses were shot from under him. He was the only officer left to help the gravely wounded commander.

Thirty years later, Washington still vividly remembered the "horror" of the battle and desperate night retreat that followed: "The dead, the dying, the groans, the lamentation, and crys along the Road of the wounded for help…were enough to pierce a heart of adamant." The frightened remnants of the once-mighty army retreated all the way to Philadelphia, leaving the Virginia frontier naked to attack.

Washington made his way back to Williamsburg, finding the capital stunned by the catastrophe. But whatever people said of Braddock's stubborn arrogance or the disgraceful panic of the regulars, no one had anything but praise for George Washington. A high-ranking English survivor declared that the colonial officer had displayed "the greatest courage and resolution." A sermon delivered in Virginia two months later (and soon published in London and the colonies) even contained a hint of prophecy: "I may point out to the Public that heroic Youth Col. Washington, who I cannot but hope Providence has hitherto preserved in so signal a Manner for some important Service to his Country." Governor Dinwiddie quickly reappointed him colonel commanding the Regiment. George Washington had won the military reputation that Americans would remember when they looked among themselves for a champion twenty years later.

The action on the Monongahela seemed to confirm not only Washington's courage but also the extraordinary good luck he enjoyed when the bullets flew. Young men tend to believe themselves invulnerable, but it is always young men that war consumes most greedily. In Washington's case the common illusion of invulnerability was to prove uncommonly durable. He had already survived several dangerous actions. From the general

George Washington, address of the officers of the Virginia Regiment to the Earl of Loudoun, July 25, 1756.
(Huntington Library: LO 1354)
At the age of only twenty-two, Washington assumed command of Virginia's troops. Although the young soldier had little military experience, he was driven by a burning desire to win distinction. In this address to the new British commander, Washington emphasized his Virginia Regiment's fighting record: "We were the first Troops in Action on the Continent…by several Engagements and continual Skirmishes with the Enemy, We have to our Cost acquired a Knowledge of Them." Colonel Washington's flamboyant six-inch-long signature hints at his fierce ambition.

massacre at the Forks, Washington wrote, "The miraculous care of Providence...protected me beyond all human expectation." Whether miraculous, providential, or merely lucky, his good fortune would continue through many years to come.

But the next three years would not be fortunate ones for Washington as he struggled to defend three hundred fifty miles of frontier with scant resources and a few hundred unreliable militiamen. Certain deficiencies were discernible in the colonel himself. His remarkable energy seemed to be employed most fervently in the cause of his own advancement. Some of his bitterest battles were waged against the British military establishment and the authorities in Williamsburg. He often lost control of his terrible temper. He bridled at any criticism. He disobeyed and intrigued against his superiors and tried to shift blame to others. He continued to campaign for a royal commission. He complained constantly about his rank and pay, inferior supplies and weapons, his treatment in the Williamsburg press, problems with the regulars and militia of other colonies, his worthless soldiers, and the igno-

George Washington, autograph letter to the Earl of Loudoun, January 10, 1757.
(Huntington Library: LO 2659)
Near the end of this fifty-page letter to his commander, Washington appealed again for a rank in the regular British army ("a better Establishment"). Washington reminded Lord Loudoun of two battles in which he had fought heroically—"our Defense at the Meadows, and behaviour under His Excellency General Braddock." But the Virginia militia colonel never received the regular army commission he wanted so much.

George Washington, autograph diagram ("Plan of a line of March"), October 8, 1758.

(Pierpont Morgan Library: MA 878)

Four years of frontier warfare gave Washington broad experience in commanding troops in battle. The young officer drafted this elaborate "Plan of a line of March" for the commanding general in his last campaign in 1758. The deployment was designed to protect a column moving through the forest against the kind of attack that had overwhelmed Braddock's army in 1755.

rance, malice, and bad judgment of the authorities—even those to whom he addressed his complaints. He threatened resignation at least seven times.

Yet the skirmishes he fought on the frontiers and in the government chambers at Williamsburg gave George Washington experience that would serve his country well in the Revolution. Few officers of Washington's age have exercised so important an independent command for so long a period. He had proved his ability to lead and had gained confidence in himself. The young soldier confronted not only the white-hot madness of battle itself, but the tedious routines of military administration. In such matters, Washington would one day display an aptitude bordering on genius. His experiences also taught him that militia troops—local volunteers serving limited enlistments—could never match regular

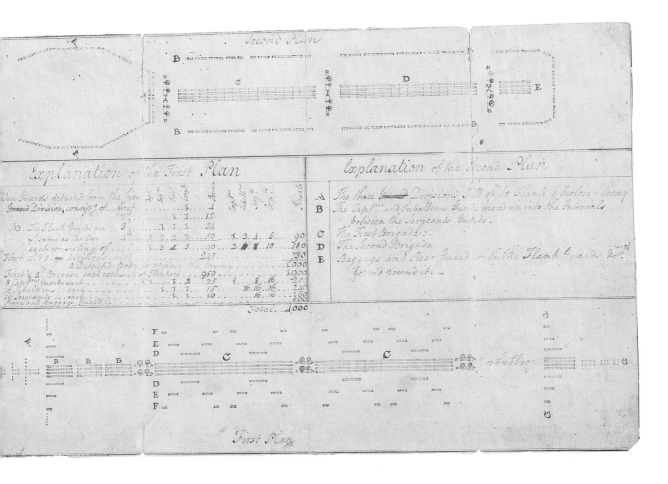

soldiers. But he understood that an American commander must make war with American soldiers.

Finally, at the end of 1758, a renewed offensive succeeded in dislodging France from the Forks of the Ohio. In this campaign Washington acted as a brigadier general, commanding two regiments. He again escaped unhurt when musket fire dropped men all around him. But with Virginia's great objective secured, Colonel Washington could hope for no further military advancement. He sent a farewell address to his officers and resigned his commission. He hoped "to find more happiness in retirement than I ever experiencd amidst a wide and bustling World." He was twenty-six years old.

Potomac Planter

———◆•••◆———

THE KEY to the happiness George Washington hoped to find in retirement at Mount Vernon was that he was now "fixd at this Seat with an agreable Consort for Life." The soldier had taken a wife. The young widow Martha Dandridge Custis had exchanged vows with him on January 6, 1759. She brought to the marriage two children—John Parke Custis, aged four, and Martha Parke Custis, two.

Martha was a few months older than George. She was also far richer. Indeed, Mrs. Custis may have been the richest marriageable woman in Virginia when the celebrated colonel first reined up at her door. Her husband had left nearly eighteen thousand fertile acres, tens of thousands of pounds, and three hundred slaves. A third of the fortune went outright to Mrs. Washington's new husband; he would control the rest until the Custis children came of age. With the several thousand acres he held in his own right, this was wealth enough to propel Washington into the highest ranks of Virginia's elite. Taking a seat in the House of Burgesses confirmed his status.

George Washington, autograph document ("Invoice of sundries to be shipd by Robert Cary and Company"), September 20, 1759.

(Huntington Library: HM 5244) George Washington married the wealthy young widow Martha Dandridge Custis on January 6, 1759. She brought to the marriage two little children—John Parke Custis and Martha Parke Custis. Washington was living at Mount Vernon with his new family when he sent to London for toys and clothing for the children.

Probably no other Virginian in the colony's history had risen as far and as fast as George Washington had between 1752 and 1759. The poorly educated younger son of a minor planter had become one of the richest and most famous men in America. Even if he did nothing else with the rest of his life, Washington had secured a good measure of the glory he had always coveted.

The next few years were, in fact, uneventful. He began life with his new family at Mount Vernon, which he had inherited after the deaths of Lawrence Washington's infant daughter and widow. All the surviving evidence—Martha would later burn most of their correspondence—suggests that the marriage was a happy one, from which both partners took strength. Wealth had played no inconsiderable part in Washington's enchantment with Mrs. Custis, while the practical widow stood to gain not only a famous husband but also a shrewd steward for her estates and a guardian for her children. More than expediency was involved, however. Man and woman were young, healthy, and attractive, and they shared a common outlook on life. It is unlikely that either harbored more than the customary share of doubts on the wedding day. In the winter of his life, Washington would advise a young relation contemplating marriage that "love is a mighty pretty thing; but like all other delicious things, it is cloying...too dainty a food to live upon *alone*." A successful marriage, he suggested, must be based on "esteem and regard," on the "friendship" that George and Martha Washington enjoyed throughout their years together.

No children were born to the couple at Mount Vernon. If Washington deeply regretted the lack, he never said so. He devoted his efforts to planting, local politics, and land speculation. His first objective was to gain the honor and riches that came with raising fine tobacco and selling it in London. It was to plant more tobacco that he began buying up adjoining lands with his new wealth.

And he bought more slaves to work his land. At the time of his marriage Washington owned about twenty slaves. That year he bought another thirteen. By the end of 1760 he owned fifty. A decade later, a Fairfax County tax roll revealed that the number had grown to ninety. Most of these people were purchased, and many came directly from the holds of slave ships that had made the horrific Atlantic crossing. Changes in agricultural practices meant that Washington bought no more slaves after 1772, but the Mount Vernon population continued to grow rapidly through natural increase.

George Washington, autograph manuscript (diary leaf), April, 1766.

(Huntington Library: HM 52708) Tobacco planting at Mount Vernon failed to yield the returns Washington had expected. He began to look around for a replacement for the traditional Virginia staple, testing scores of crops before deciding to substitute wheat for tobacco. This leaf torn from one of Washington's pocket diaries reveals that in the spring of 1766 the master of Mount Vernon was planting hemp. The fibrous plant was used in making rope and canvas.

Washington's generally decent treatment of his slaves did little to relieve the plight of a people doomed to perpetual captivity. American slavery was one of the most oppressive labor systems the western world has known. The day would come when George Washington would be profoundly troubled by his recognition of slavery's cruelty and its inevitable debasement of the society in which it flourished. But if such reflections disturbed him before the Revolution, he left no record of it. Indeed, Washington would have been a most unusual mid-eighteenth-century Virginia planter had he entertained serious doubts about a system that was so much a part of the accepted order of his world.

Success did not attend Washington's attempts to become a great tobacco planter. All his efforts to grow the quality leaf that commanded the best prices in England were frustrated by poor Mount Vernon soils, indifferent markets, British regulations, and

["Plan and section of a slave-ship," 1789], in Thomas Clarkson, *The History of the Rise, Progress, and Accomplishment of the Abolition of the African Slave Trade by the British Parliament,* London, 1808.

(Huntington Library: 297309) Africans carried across the ocean to enslavement in the Americas endured a horrific ordeal. During his expansion of Mount Vernon in the 1760s, Washington purchased many slaves—some of them direct from the holds of slave ships.

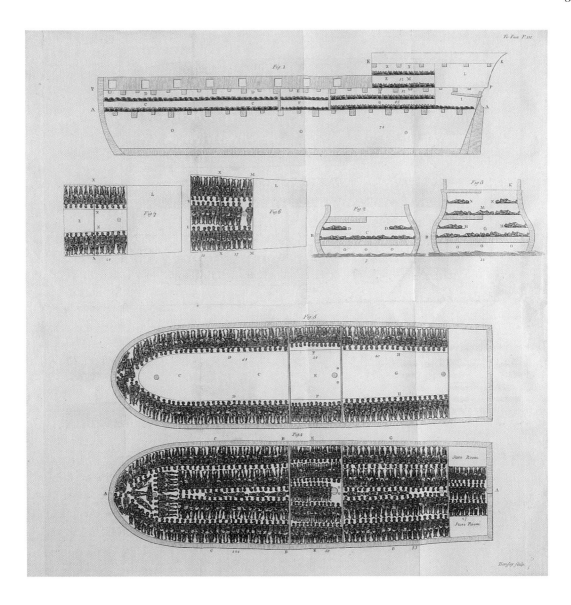

bad weather. At the same time, Washington was spending lavishly—on land, slaves, and equipment; on costly imported luxuries; and in the enjoyment of the opulence for which Virginia plantation culture is still renowned. Annual tobacco crops consigned for sale to his London agents failed to offset the cost of goods ordered on credit from those same trading houses. He spent up the wealth gained by his marriage and began to run into debt, a circumstance he abhorred as both bad business and a slight on his honor. Washington became increasingly embittered by the sharp practices of English merchants, and by his growing conviction that the imperial system exploited colonials.

His military experiences had done much to disabuse this subject of the Crown of his youthful devotion to the mother country. He had complained during his fruitless quest for a regular army commission that "we cannot conceive that because we are Americans, we shou'd *therefore* be deprived of the Benefits common to British Subjects." His treatment at the hands of the London traders only strengthened this tendency to think of himself as an American. His failure to gain the rewards he thought the British military establishment owed him had soured Washington on a society in which success was based not so much on merit as on "interest"—the influence of the powerful. Such considerations may well have made him more open to republican ideals, and, one day, to the radical notion of independent American nationhood.

But it was economic, not political, independence that Washington pursued in the 1760s. As many of his Virginia neighbors sank into a pit of tobacco debt from which they would never crawl free, George Washington set out, with characteristic energy, to find a replacement for the traditional staple crop. He began the agricultural experimentation that absorbed him for the rest of his life. He tested dozens of crops before settling on wheat as the main replacement for soil-depleting tobacco. Washington would gain a reputation as one of the most progressive large-scale farmers in America. It was a new infusion of Custis wealth, however, that finally allowed him to cancel his English debts. When "our Dear Patcy Custis" died during an epileptic seizure in 1773, her stepfather inherited £8,000.

Washington would spend fifteen years as a gentleman planter at Mount Vernon between his two wars. It was the longest stretch of private life he would ever enjoy, and certainly the happiest period of his life. His other preoccupation was speculation in western land. In 1763 the Seven Years' War had finally come to an end. England had gained a prodigious victory. The choicest por-

Virginia, ff.

By the Hon. *ROBERT DINWIDDIE*, Efq; His Majefty's Lieutenant-Governor, and Commander in Chief of this Dominion.

A PROCLAMATION,

For Encouraging MEN to enlift in his Majefty's Service for the Defence and Security of this Colony.

WHEREAS it is determined that a Fort be immediately built on the River *Ohio*, at the Fork of *Monongahela*, to oppofe any further Encroachments, or hoftile Attempts of the *French*, and the *Indians* in their Intereft, and for the Security and Protection of his Majefty's Subjects in this Colony; and as it is abfolutely neceffary that a fufficient Force fhould be raifed to erect and fupport the fame: For an Encouragement to all who fhall voluntarily enter into the faid Service, I do hereby notify and promife, by and with the Advice and Confent of his Majefty's Council of this Colony, that over and above their Pay, Two Hundred Thoufand Acres, of his Majefty the King of *Great-Britain*'s Lands, on the Eaft Side of the River *Ohio*, within this Dominion, (One Hundred Thoufand Acres whereof to be contiguous to the faid Fort, and the other Hundred Thoufand Acres to be on, or near the River *Ohio*) fhall be laid off and granted to fuch Perfons, who by their voluntary Engagement, and good Behaviour in the faid Service, fhall deferve the fame. And I further promife, that the faid Lands fhall be divided amongft them immediately after the Performance of the faid Service, in a Proportion due to their refpective Merit, as fhall be reprefented to me by their Officers, and held and enjoyed by them without paying any Rights, and alfo free from the Payment of Quit-rents, for the Term of Fifteen Years. And I do appoint this Proclamation to be read and publifhed at the Court-Houfes, Churches and Chapels in each County within this Colony, and that the Sheriffs take Care the fame be done accordingly.

Given at the Council-Chamber in *Williamsburg*, on the 19th Day of *February*, in the 27th Year of his Majefty's Reign, *Annoque Domini* 1754.

ROBERT DINWIDDIE.

GOD Save the KING.

Robert Dinwiddie, *A Proclamation… February 19, 1754,* Williamsburg, 1754.

(Huntington Library: 19867)

The governor of Virginia promised two hundred thousand acres of bounty land to encourage soldiers to enlist in the campaign to drive France from the Ohio Valley. After the French were defeated, George Washington used the governor's grant to add tens of thousands of acres of prime western land to his own holdings.

tion of the victor's spoils was Canada and the Ohio Valley. With the French ousted and their Indian allies bereft of a European partner, rich visions again floated above the western horizon.

No one had grander visions than George Washington. In 1754, Washington had built the primitive road that opened the Ohio Valley to wheeled vehicles for the first time. By the 1770s he had realized that the construction of a system of canals and roads linking the Potomac and Ohio was within the grasp of existing technologies. He was convinced that the Ohio Valley contained the finest agricultural land on earth. If its harvests could be funneled to the world's markets on the river that flowed past Mount Vernon, the value of Washington's western lands was certain to climb to the skies. And Alexandria, just a few miles from his door, stood to become the greatest trading port in America. Washington pursued the western land with the same drive that had carried him over miles of hostile terrain and through a half-dozen deadly battles.

When Major Washington returned to Williamsburg with

George Washington, autograph letter to Jonathan Boucher, May 5, 1772.

(Huntington Library: HM 5274) Washington worked for decades to promote the creation of a system of canals and roads to link the Potomac and Ohio rivers. As this letter reveals, he recognized that moving the harvests of the Ohio Valley east across the mountains would produce "amazing advantages" for Virginia. Another likely result would be an amazing increase in the value of Washington's western lands.

news of the French challenge in January 1754, Governor Dinwiddie had issued a proclamation promising two hundred thousand acres of western land as bounty to soldiers who enlisted in the campaign to drive the enemy from the Forks of the Ohio. Historians have questioned whether commissioned officers, who were not enlisted soldiers, were eligible to share in the original grant. But in 1770, Washington successfully petitioned to have the bounty extended to officers.

Fifteen thousand acres each was the allotment reserved for

Silver-handled knife and fork.

(National Museum of American History, Smithsonian Institution: 13152; 1198)

This knife and fork from a silver service that George Washington ordered from London in 1757 are engraved with the Washington family crest.

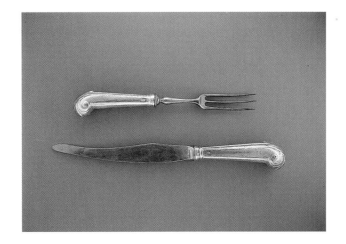

Blue and white Chinese porcelain export platter.

(National Museum of American History, Smithsonian Institution: 13152; 1177)

An example of the Chinese export china that Martha Washington called "the ware in common use" at Mount Vernon.

Washington and his field officers. An enlisted man could expect just four hundred acres. With the purchase of other veterans' claims added to his own share, Washington eventually acquired about thirty thousand acres along the Ohio and Kanawha rivers in what is now West Virginia. When some complained that Washington's portion contained most of the prime bottomland, he retorted, with some accuracy, that without "my unremitting attention to every circumstance, not a single acre of Land ever would have been obtained."

But Washington knew that his western land would never be valuable unless the Ohio was settled and joined, politically and economically, to the seaboard colonies. His stake in the west enlarged his hopes for himself and his country to a continental scale.

Amber necklace owned by Martha Washington.
(National Museum of American History, Smithsonian Institution: 319870.1)
George Washington's account books reveal that he bought jewelry for Martha during every year of their marriage.

"Because We Are Americans"

———◆◆◆———

ON THE AFTERNOON of September 4, 1774, George Washington rode into Philadelphia and stopped at the City Tavern. Virginia had elected him one of its delegates to the first Continental Congress, the meeting called to seek a united colonial response to the crisis that was rapidly driving America to war with Britain. War was now only months away.

With some twenty-five thousand inhabitants, Philadelphia was the largest city in North America. On his first trip to the great metropolis, in 1757, Colonel Washington had met with a humiliating rejection of his appeal for a royal army commission. By 1774 the mission had changed, and so had George Washington. In the years since the war against the French, Washington had won his most important victory—the feat that one fellow revolutionary described as Washington's victory over himself. The jealous, hot-tempered, selfish young officer who had so relentlessly crusaded for his own advancement had become a mature patriot whose private ambitions were now sublimated in his devotion to a higher cause. That cause, Washington and his compatriots believed, was nothing less than the preservation of liberty itself.

The militancy of George Washington's political views have not always been recognized. If Washington moved reluctantly toward rebellion and independence, his ideas were more advanced than those of most colonials. As early as 1769 he predicted in a letter to a friend that "our lordly Masters in Great Britain will be satisfied with nothing less than the deprivation of American freedom." He declared that "no man shou'd scruple, or hesitate a moment to use a[r]ms in defense of so valuable a blessing." To speak of war with Britain at that early date was radical indeed. And certainly no man in America better understood how dangerous such a war must be.

The fierce denunciation of "our lordly Masters" was drawn from Washington's pen by taxes levied on the colonies by the British Parliament. When the Seven Years' War ended, England learned that victory had been as costly as it had been glorious. In 1763, British national debt stood at an appalling £122,603,336. London concluded that the Americans had profited most from the war and that they could afford some of its cost. A stubborn new monarch had ascended the English throne in 1760, and King George III and his government vowed to bring the ungrateful Americans under the control of rightful British authority.

The imperial crisis broke out with Parliament's passage in 1765 of the Stamp Act, which levied taxes on the colonies. In the minds of colonials, the Stamp Act conjured up frightful visions of dark conspiracy and limitless tyrannies to follow. Property rights were central to the Americans' notions of freedom. They believed that taxation without their consent amounted to the theft of their property, and thus a first step on the road to absolute slavery. Washington was united with other patriots in opposition to what he called "this unconstitutional method of Taxation" that Virginians viewed as a "direful attack upon their Liberties."

Other Americans greeted the Stamp Act not with dignified

appeals to tradition but with mob violence, boycotts, and tax evasion. In the face of such defiance, the law proved unenforceable and was repealed in 1766 to universal rejoicing throughout the colonies. Respect for British authority would never be the same, even though the king's determination to rule the unruly colonials was stronger than ever.

Americans were outraged anew by the passage of the Townshend Acts in 1767. The bill was intended to raise revenues for the Crown by collecting duties on imports. Colonials countered with "nonimportation," the boycott of trade with Britain. By 1769, Washington had emerged as a leader of the nonimportation

Paul Revere, *The Bloody Massacre perpetrated in . . . Boston on March 5th 1770. . . . , Boston, 1770.*

(Gilder Lehrman Collection, on deposit at the Pierpont Morgan Library: GLC01868)

The famous silversmith's spirited depiction of the Boston massacre remains the most effective piece of war propaganda in American history. Boston led the resistance to Britain's attempts to tax and rule the colonies in the decade before the outbreak of the American Revolution.

movement in Fairfax County, the most radical county in Virginia, a colony that was itself among the most outspoken in opposition to British authority.

But Boston remained the crucible of American resistance. Boston was a port built on trade, as well as a hotbed of radical patriotism. Here opposition to import taxes and dishonest tax collectors was often violent. To bring the Bostonians into line, British troops occupied the city in 1768. The appearance of a standing army during peacetime only confirmed Americans' worst fears

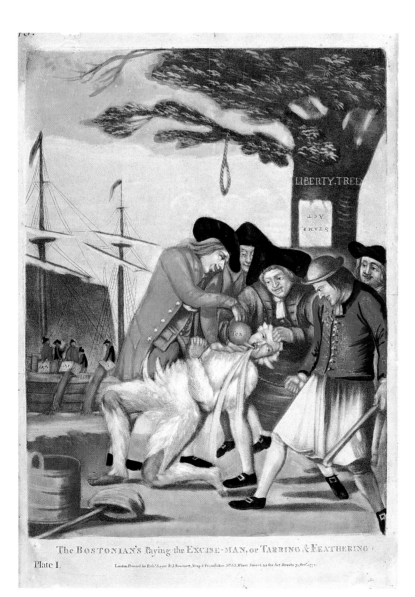

The Bostonian's Paying the EXCISE-MAN, or TARRING & FEATHERING

Plate I.   London, Printed for Robt Sayer & J Bennett, Map & Printsellers No 53, Fleet Street, as the Act directs 30 Oct 1774.

The Bostonians Paying the Excise-Man or Tarring & Feathering, London, 1774.

(Gilder Lehrman Collection, on deposit at the Pierpont Morgan Library: GLC04961.01) Massachusetts civic leaders urge a British official to consider a tax reform program while their colleagues turn Boston harbor into the world's largest teapot. The Boston Tea Party of December 1773 infuriated official London. Parliament swiftly passed the harsh Coercive Acts that pushed Massachusetts into open rebellion.

about the conspiracy to rob them of their liberties. Hatred between soldiers and townspeople erupted in the Boston Massacre in 1770, when redcoats fired into a rioting crowd, killing five. Parliament finally repealed most of the Townshend duties, retaining only a three-penny-a-pound tax on tea. But even this proved too much for angry Bostonians to swallow. On December 16, 1773, a band of patriots unconvincingly disguised as Mohawks destroyed fifty tons of British property while turning Boston harbor into the world's biggest teapot.

The Boston Tea Party infuriated official London. Nearly everyone now agreed that Massachusetts had to be broken before England's American empire was lost forever. Parliament quickly passed the laws known in the colonies as the Coercive or Intolerable Acts. The Boston Port Bill closed the harbor to trade, inflicting grave economic hardship. The action amounted to the kind of naval blockade that warring nations employed against their enemies.

The Massachusetts Government Act abrogated the colony's 1691 charter. General Thomas Gage, British North American commander, was appointed royal governor of Massachusetts. More of the hated redcoats trooped ashore from warships in the harbor. But since Gage's regiments were confined to Boston, British authority ended at city limits. His Majesty's ancient plantation of Massachusetts-Bay had edged into open rebellion.

News of the Intolerable Acts reached Williamsburg when Washington was attending the Assembly. On May 26, 1774, the Burgesses passed a resolution calling for a day of fasting and prayer to protest this "heavy Calamity, which threatens Destruction to our civil Rights, and the Evils of Civil War." The governor promptly dissolved the Assembly. Just as promptly, the delegates reassembled in a tavern and continued debate in an extralegal session. They proclaimed solidarity with Massachusetts and called for a "general congress" of "the several Colonies of British America."

The British plan to divide the colonies by punishing only Massachusetts had failed. Washington declared that "the cause of Boston [is] the cause of America," and his sentiments were shared by all patriots. Earlier than most colonists, Washington had concluded that further appeals to king and Parliament were futile: neither side would back down, and Americans could choose only between surrender and resistance. King George agreed. "The dye is now cast," he told his prime minister. "The Colonies must either submit or triumph."

In July 1774, Washington chaired a mass meeting at the Fairfax County Court House at which a series of influential resolutions—the Fairfax Resolves—were adopted. These resolutions affirmed the Americans' right to govern themselves and organized a new boycott of British trade. Ominously, the twenty-third resolution warned that, if the king continued to ignore demands for justice, "there can be but one Appeal"—the appeal to arms.

PREMIÈRE ASSEMBLÉE DU CONGRÈS.

"Assemblée Du Congrès," in M. Hilliard D'Auberteuil, *Essais Historiques et Politiques sur les Anglo-Americans*, Brussels, 1781.

(Huntington Library: 140869)

In 1774, Washington attended the First Continental Congress in Philadelphia. This imaginary French depiction of Congress in session appeared in 1781.

When the delegates to the Congress met in Philadelphia in September 1774, they were pleased to discover that leaders from diverse colonies were in agreement on many issues. They also took one another's measure. Some who knew Washington only by reputation were surprised by the forty-two-year-old's youthfulness. They had assumed that a man who had held so high a rank in the "French war" to be a decade or two older. The Congress passed a resolution declaring that colonial assemblies, not Parliament, retained "exclusive power of legislation...in all cases of taxation and internal polity" in America.

The folly of king and Parliament had driven the Americans from a principled denial of Parliament's right to tax them to an outright rejection of any Parliamentary authority. The British had unwittingly framed the debate as a choice between complete subordination to or complete independence from Parliament's control. Very well, the Americans responded, we choose independence. Patriot leaders now claimed in effect a commonwealth status, in which, as members of the British Empire, they might grant loyalty to the king but owed no obedience to Parliament. London, of course, greeted such interpretations with indignation. The Americans were in rebellion and they would be crushed by British power.

Massachusetts had already felt British power by the time the second Continental Congress met in Philadelphia, in May 1775. Parliament formally declared Massachusetts to be in a state of rebellion. General Gage was ordered to move against the rebels. He sent a raiding party into enemy territory, which by now comprised most of the thirteen colonies. Gage's objective was the gunpowder stored at Concord, a few miles outside Boston. No gunpowder was confiscated, but both sides managed to explode quantities of it that day—the momentous "19th of April" 1775. The morning's first volleys swept the minutemen from Lexington Green, but in the hours that followed, the redcoats paid the price. Resurgent militia poured fire into the regulars' ranks and sent them reeling back into the arms of the relief column that saved them from annihilation. Thousands of armed patriots from throughout New England ringed Boston, besieging Gage's regiments.

In June 1775 the king's men had a chance to redeem themselves. The patriots tightened their grip on the city by seizing Bunker Hill, a commanding eminence just across the water. The British resolved to drive them off. In certain circumstances, firearms can give untrained men an edge over regular soldiers. The battle of Bunker Hill produced just such a circumstance for the Americans. For the British, the battle produced little but carnage. They finally forced the Americans from the hill, but only after leaving one thousand soldiers—nearly half their number—dead and wounded on the bloody slopes leading to the rebel redoubt. A few more such "victories" and Britain would have no army left in Boston. In the future, His Majesty's generals would be disinclined to order frontal assaults on fortified rebel positions.

George Washington had impressed his fellow delegates at the first Congress. They admired not only his youthful bearing but also his calm judgment and his unswerving commitment to the American cause. They recognized in him an astute politician and a practiced legislator. The Virginian made an even stronger impression at the second Congress, when he entered the Pennsylvania State House wearing his militia colonel's uniform. Standing a tow-

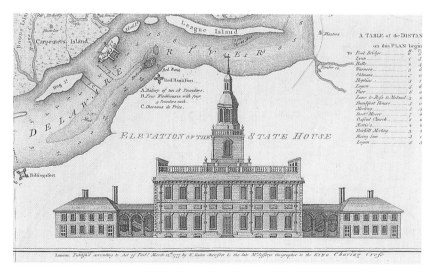

"Elevation of the State House," detail from *A Plan of the City and Environs of Philadelphia . . .* **London, March 12, 1777.**

(Huntington Library: 129340)

On June 15, 1775, Congress appointed Washington a full general, commanding the new Continental Army, in the Pennsylvania State House (later known as Independence Hall).

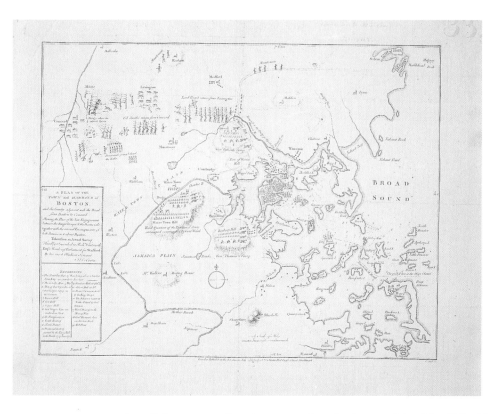

J. DeCosta, *A Plan of the Town and Harbour of Boston . . . with the Road from Boston to Concord Shewing the Place of the late Engagement between the King's Troops & the Provincials . . .* , **London, July 29, 1775.**

(Huntington Library: Museum Map Store Collection, 93/578)

The American Revolution began with the fighting at Lexington and Concord on April 19, 1775. This rare map is the earliest published depiction of the first battle of the Revolutionary War. American minutemen nearly wiped out the British raiding party sent out from Boston to seize military supplies.

ering 6-feet-3, a glittering sword swinging at his side, Washington looked magnificent. The uniform signified both his rank in the Virginia militia and his readiness to risk his life as the men of Massachusetts had done. Washington and the other delegates knew that all hope of peaceful resolution had died at Lexington. He wrote that now the "once happy and peaceful plains of America are either to be drenched with Blood, or Inhabited by Slaves." Did the uniform also signal Washington's willingness to assume high command in the coming struggle?

On June 14, Congress declared that the collection of New England militia companies camped outside Boston was now the Continental Army. The next day the delegates named Washington its supreme commander, bumping up the Virginia colonel four grades, to full general, with a flourish of oratory. At the same time, Congress had affirmed the Revolution's continental scope by giving the New England army a southern chief. Washington accepted the commission. But he told his colleagues that "I feel great distress,

In Congress

To George Washington Esq.

This Congress having appointed you to be General
& Commander in chief of the army of the United Colonies
and of all the forces raised or to be raised by them and of all others
who shall voluntarily offer their service and join the said army,
for the defence of American liberty and for repelling every hostile
invasion thereof, you are to repair with all expedition to the
colony of Massachussetts-bay and take charge of the army
of the United Colonies.

For your better direction

First   You are to make a return to us, as soon as possible of all
forces, which you shall have under your command, together
with their military stores and provisions; and also as exact an
account as you can obtain of the forces which compose the
British army in America.

Secondly.   You are not to disband any of the men you find raised
until further direction from this Congress; and if you shall think
their numbers not adequate to the purpose of security, you may
recruit them to a number you shall think sufficient not exceeding
double that of the enemy.

Thirdly.   In all cases of vacancy occasioned by death or a removal
of a Colonel or other inferior officer, you are by Brevet or Warrant
under your seal to appoint another person to fill up such
vacancy, until it shall be otherwise ordered by the provincial Convention or Assembly of the colony, from whence the troops,
in which such vacancy happen, shall direct otherwise. —

Fourthly,   You are to victual at the continental expence all such
volunteers as have joined, or shall join the united army.

Fifthly.

Fifthly. You shall take every method in your power consistent with prudence, to destroy or make prisoners of all persons, who now are, or who hereafter shall appear in arms against the good people of the United Colonies.

Sixthly. And whereas all particulars cannot be foreseen, nor positive instructions for such emergencies so beforehand given, but that many things must be left to your prudent and discreet management, as occurrences may arise upon the place or from time to time fallout; You are, therefore, upon all such accidents or any occasion, that may happen, to use your best circumspection and (advising with your council of war) to order and dispose of the said army under your command, as may be most advantageous for the obtaining the end for which these forces have been raised, making it your special care, in discharge of the great trust committed unto you, that the liberties of America receive no detriment.

Philadelphia June 22: 1775
By Order of Congress,
John Hancock President

In addition to ye Instructions it is Resolved by Congress, That the troops including the volunteers be furnished with camp equipage & blankets if necessary at the Continental expence

That the officers now in the army receive their commissions from the Genl. or commander in chief praying milled

That a sum not exceeding two millions of dollars be emitted by the Congress in bills of credit for the defence of America

Cha. Thomson Secry —
By Order of Congress
John Hancock President

from a consciousness that my abilities & Military experience may not be equal to the extensive & important Trust.... I do not think myself equal to the Command I am honoured with." He refused any salary, asking only that his expenses be met.

Historians have long debated Washington's reasons for accepting the command, apparently against his better judgment. Was it concern for his honor that obliged a reluctant Washington to assume a burden he never wanted? This was certainly the reason the new general gave his anxious wife, waiting for him at Mount Vernon: "You may believe me my dear Patcy, when I assure you, in the most solemn manner, that, so far from seeking this appointment, I have used every endeavor in my power to avoid it.... But, as it has been a kind of destiny, that has thrown me upon this Service, I shall hope that my undertaking it is designd to answer some good purpose.... It was utterly out of my power to refuse this appointment without exposing my Character to such censures as would have reflected dishonour upon myself."

But such explanations do not always reflect the true wishes of those who offer them. George Washington wanted the command. His ambition demanded nothing less, and he was too good a politician not to know that the appointment would probably be his. One simple fact is often overlooked: Washington must have suspected that no other American was more qualified than he to lead the army of the united colonies. If he truly wanted to preserve American liberty, he could make but one decision. As he put it himself, "Can a virtuous Man hesitate in his choice?" Of course, he had to exercise caution—the smallest hint that he had sought power would alarm a people so jealous of their liberties, so fearful of tyrants. Congress had picked one of its own, a gentleman of substantial fortune. His fellow delegates knew him well enough to trust that George Washington stood before them in the uniform of a patriot, not a military usurper.

Washington's duty to what he called the "glorious cause" and his hopes for himself had become two sides of the same coin.

Previous pages

Continental Congress, manuscript instructions ("To George Washington, Esq.") signed twice by John Hancock, June 22, 1775.

(Huntington Library: HM 22011) "Congress having appointed you to be General & Commander in Chief of the army of the United Colonies...for the defense of American liberty." General Washington received these first orders from Congress the day before he left Philadelphia to take command of the American forces outside Boston. The thousands of untrained volunteers he found at Cambridge were an army in name only.

Martha Washington, autograph letter to Elizabeth Ramsey, December 30, 1775.

(Pierpont Morgan Library: MA 1008)

Martha Washington joined her husband at the Continental Army's winter quarters every year of the war. She passed the winter of 1775–76 outside Boston, where the American army was besieging the British regiments in the city. In this letter to a friend in Virginia, Mrs. Washington reported that "some days we have a number of Cannon and shells from Boston and Bunkers Hill, but it does not seem to surprise any one but me; I confess I shudder every time I hear the sound of a gun." The general's wife was also surprised that she had been treated with "great pomp as if I had been a very great somebody."

For he was contending now for the prize that surpassed all others—more brilliant than any rank or title, more alluring than a rich wife or an opulent plantation, more enduring than power itself. If he could achieve victory over the might of Great Britain, the General stood to win the kind of fame that outlasts the centuries. Washington's yearning for honor burned as brightly as ever. Only now his highest aspiration was the success of the American cause, for that success would bring George Washington as much of immortality as fame can ever give.

At the same time, Washington's fears were unfeigned. "I

am now Imbarked on a tempestuous Ocean," he wrote a friend a few days after his appointment, "from whence, perhaps, no friendly harbour is to be found." He reportedly had tears in his eyes when he revealed to Patrick Henry, just after his appointment, that "from the day I entered upon the command of the American armies, I date my fall, and the ruin of my reputation." Washington, a former militia officer who twenty years before had commanded small bodies of men with limited success, was now charged with leading an entire army against one of the most formidable powers on earth.

He set off for Boston with a copy of his instructions from the Continental Congress, boldly signed by John Hancock. He took command at Cambridge, and the next day, July 4, 1775, issued his first orders. Washington told the men that they were now the army of the "United Provinces of North America; and it is hoped that all Distinctions of Colonies will be laid aside." But the commander in chief knew that the crowd of some fifteen thousand undisciplined militiamen was an army only because Congress designated it one. He puzzled over how they could be molded into an effective fighting force.

The siege of Boston continued through the winter. Washington proposed risking the army in a mass attack; his generals dissuaded him. Finally, in March 1776, the Americans placed heavy artillery on the heights above the city. The British evacuated Boston. Despite American rejoicing, it was an empty victory: the enemy had left Boston only in order to win the war elsewhere. Although British conduct of the war was never distinguished by strategic brilliance, or even by much strategic coherence, the high command did understand that Boston, far to the north, was not a suitable base from which to undertake the subjugation of the colonies. When the fleet carrying England's regiments sailed out of Boston harbor, both sides knew that New York City would be the next objective. And disaster awaited Washington and his untried army at New York.

Winter Soldier

———————◆●◆●◆———————

HE CONTINENTAL ARMY reached New York in April 1776. Washington had chosen to defend an indefensible city. He was outnumbered by superior troops, and New York's geography of rivers, bays, and islands gave overwhelming advantage to an enemy who possessed absolute naval superiority.

Britain's military might in North America was now wielded by two brothers—General William Howe and Admiral Lord Richard Howe. The Howes felt a genuine affection for the disaffected Americans, and they had been authorized by the home government to try for a peaceful settlement. Should such efforts fail, however, the Howe brothers were strictly charged by their sovereign king to destroy the rebellion.

All hopes of political settlement were illusory, however. By 1776, too many Americans were committed to the once-radical notion of independent nationhood. Not least among them was the commander in chief of the Continental Army. General Washington had been advocating independence for months; his actions over the past year had already done much to push his country in

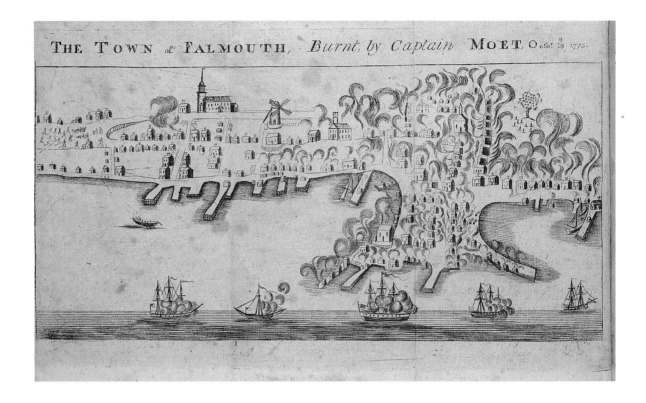

that direction. But the British themselves had done far more. The king to whom Americans appealed had harshly condemned his subjects as traitors and rebels. His Majesty's soldiers and sailors had attacked American commerce, destroyed property, even burned whole towns, including Norfolk, Virginia, and Falmouth, Massachusetts. They had armed southern slaves against their masters and sent Indians surging across the western frontiers. Killing is carried forward by its own inexorable logic; few were ready to forgive in 1776.

"A few more such flaming Arguments as were exhibited at Falmouth and Norfolk, added to the sound Doctrine, and unanswerable reasoning contain (in the pamphlet) Common Sense" would soon convince Americans to seek independence, Washington predicted. In January 1776, Washington and thousands of others had discovered "sound Doctrine" within the pages of Thomas Paine's *Common Sense*. Paine urged his readers to embrace not just

"The Town of Falmouth, Burnt by Captain Moet, Octbr. 18th 1775," in *Impartial History of the War in America*, **Boston, 1782.**

(Huntington Library: 180000) General Washington was outraged by British destruction of American coastal towns like Falmouth, Massachusetts. It helped convince him that the Americans should seek complete independence from Great Britain.

Thomas Paine, *Common Sense...*, Philadelphia, 1776.

(Huntington Library: 92574)

Tom Paine appealed to Americans' growing conviction that they were a people chosen to lead the world to liberty. Washington was one of the tens of thousands of readers who found Paine's eloquence persuasive.

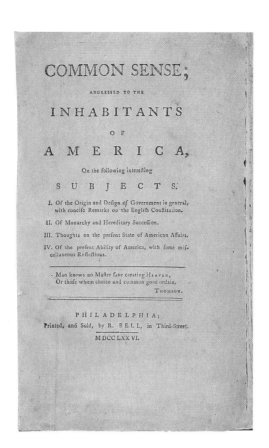

COMMON SENSE;

ADDRESSED TO THE

INHABITANTS

OF

AMERICA,

On the following interesting

S U B J E C T S.

I. Of the Origin and Design of Government in general, with concise Remarks on the English Constitution.

II. Of Monarchy and Hereditary Succession.

III. Thoughts on the present State of American Affairs.

IV. Of the present Ability of America, with some miscellaneous Reflections.

Man knows no Master save creating HEAVEN,
Or those whom choice and common good ordain.

THOMSON.

PHILADELPHIA;

Printed, and Sold, by R. BELL, in Third-Street.

M DCC LXX VI.

independence but a new era of history. "We have it in our power to begin the world over again," he insisted.

Tom Paine condemned government by birth and sentenced it to death. Monarchy and aristocracy were evils surviving from a savage past. The time had come to destroy hereditary power, and that high destiny belonged to the Americans. Paine appealed to their growing conviction that they were a people chosen to lead the world to liberty. "The cause of America," he assured them, "is in a great measure the cause of all mankind." Paine was right. The future that the American Revolution inaugurated would eventually tumble Europe's proud ones into political obscurity. The war that was just beginning in 1776 would transcend the contest for colonial independence to become a mighty revolution waged in the name of human equality.

And so, as the Continental Army awaited battle on Long

In CONGRESS, July 4, 1776.

A DECLARATION

By the REPRESENTATIVES of the

UNITED STATES OF AMERICA,

In GENERAL CONGRESS ASSEMBLED.

WHEN in the Course of human Events, it becomes neceffary for one People to diffolve the Political Bands which have connected them with another, and to affume among the Powers of the Earth, the feparate and equal Station to which the Laws of Nature and of Nature's God entitle them, a decent Refpect to the Opinions of Mankind requires that they fhould declare the caufes which impel them to the Separation.

We hold thefe Truths to be felf-evident, that all Men are created equal, that they are endowed by their Creator with certain unalienable Rights, that among thefe are Life, Liberty, and the Purfuit of Happinefs—That to fecure thefe Rights, Governments are inftituted among Men, deriving their juft Powers from the Confent of the Governed, that whenever any Form of Government becomes deftructive of thefe Ends, it is the Right of the People to alter or to abolifh it, and to inftitute new Government, laying its Foundation on fuch Principles, and organizing its Powers in fuch Form, as to them fhall feem moft likely to effect their Safety and Happinefs. Prudence, indeed, will dictate that Governments long eftablifhed fhould not be changed for light and tranfient Caufes; and accordingly all Experience hath fhewn, that Mankind are more difpofed to fuffer, while Evils are fufferable, than to right themfelves by abolifhing the Forms to which they are accuftomed. But when a long Train of Abufes and Ufurpations, purfuing invariably the fame Object, evinces a Defign to reduce them under abfolute Defpotifm, it is their Right, it is their Duty, to throw off fuch Government, and to provide new Guards for their future Security. Such has been the patient Sufferance of thefe Colonies; and fuch is now the Neceffity which conftrains them to alter their former Syftems of Government. The Hiftory of the prefent King of Great-Britain is a Hiftory of repeated Injuries and Ufurpations, all having in direct Object the Eftablifhment of an abfolute Tyranny over thefe States. To prove this, let Facts be fubmitted to a candid World.

He has refufed his Affent to Laws, the moft wholefome and neceffary for the public Good.

He has forbidden his Governors to pafs Laws of immediate and preffing Importance, unlefs fufpended in their Operation till his Affent fhould be obtained; and when fo fufpended, he has utterly neglected to attend to them.

He has refufed to pafs other Laws for the Accommodation of large Diftricts of People, unlefs thofe People would relinquifh the Right of Reprefentation in the Legiflature, a Right ineftimable to them, and formidable to Tyrants only.

He has called together Legiflative Bodies at Places unufual, uncomfortable, and diftant from the Depofitory of their public Records, for the fole Purpofe of fatiguing them into Compliance with his Meafures.

He has diffolved Reprefentative Houfes repeatedly, for oppofing with manly Firmnefs his Invafions on the Rights of the People.

He has refufed for a long Time, after fuch Diffolutions, to caufe others to be elected; whereby the Legiflative Powers, incapable of Annihilation, have returned to the People at large for their exercife; the State remaining in the mean time expofed to all the Dangers of Invafion from without, and Convulfions within.

He has endeavoured to prevent the Population of thefe States; for that Purpofe obftructing the Laws for Naturalization of Foreigners; refufing to pafs others to encourage their Migrations hither, and raifing the Conditions of new Appropriations of Lands.

He has obftructed the Adminiftration of Juftice, by refufing his Affent to Laws for eftablifhing Judiciary Powers.

He has made Judges dependent on his Will alone, for the Tenure of their Offices, and the Amount and Payment of their Salaries.

He has erected a Multitude of new Offices, and fent hither Swarms of Officers to harrafs our People, and eat out their Subftance.

He has kept among us, in Times of Peace, Standing Armies, without the confent of our Legiflatures.

He has affected to render the Military independent of and fuperior to the Civil Power.

He has combined with others to fubject us to a Jurifdiction foreign to our Conftitution, and unacknowledged by our Laws; giving his Affent to their Acts of pretended Legiflation:

For quartering large Bodies of Armed Troops among us:

For protecting them, by a mock Trial, from Punifhment for any Murders which they fhould commit on the Inhabitants of thefe States:

For cutting off our Trade with all Parts of the World:

For impofing Taxes on us without our Confent:

For depriving us, in many Cafes, of the Benefits of Trial by Jury:

For tranfporting us beyond Seas to be tried for pretended Offences:

For abolifhing the free Syftem of Englifh Laws in a neighbouring Province, eftablifhing therein an arbitrary Government, and enlarging its Boundaries, fo as to render it at once an Example and fit Inftrument for introducing the fame abfolute Rule into thefe Colonies:

For taking away our Charters, abolifhing our moft valuable Laws, and altering fundamentally the Forms of our Governments:

For fufpending our own Legiflatures, and declaring themfelves invefted with Power to legiflate for us in all Cafes whatfoever.

He has abdicated Government here, by declaring us out of his Protection and waging War againft us.

He has plundered our Seas, ravaged our Coafts, burnt our Towns, and deftroyed the Lives of our People.

He is, at this Time, tranfporting large Armies of foreign Mercenaries to compleat the Works of Death, Defolation, and Tyranny, already begun with circumftances of Cruelty and Perfidy, fcarcely paralleled in the moft barbarous Ages, and totally unworthy the Head of a civilized Nation.

He has conftrained our fellow Citizens taken Captive on the high Seas to bear Arms againft their Country, to become the Executioners of their Friends and Brethren, or to fall themfelves by their Hands.

He has excited domeftic Infurrections amongft us, and has endeavoured to bring on the Inhabitants of our Frontiers, the mercilefs Indian Savages, whofe known Rule of Warfare, is an undiftinguifhed Deftruction, of all Ages, Sexes and Conditions.

In every ftage of thefe Oppreffions we have Petitioned for Redrefs in the moft humble Terms: Our repeated Petitions have been anfwered only by repeated Injury. A Prince, whofe Character is thus marked by every act which may define a Tyrant, is unfit to be the Ruler of a free People.

Nor have we been wanting in Attentions to our Britifh Brethren. We have warned them from Time to Time of Attempts by their Legiflature to extend an unwarrantable Jurifdiction over us. We have reminded them of the Circumftances of our Emigration and Settlement here. We have appealed to their native Juftice and Magnanimity, and we have conjured them by the Ties of our common Kindred to difavow thefe Ufurpations, which, would inevitably interrupt our Connections and Correfpondence. They too have been deaf to the Voice of Juftice and of Confanguinity. We muft, therefore, acquiefce in the Neceffity, which denounces our Separation, and hold them, as we hold the reft of Mankind, Enemies in War, in Peace, Friends.

We, therefore, the Reprefentatives of the UNITED STATES OF AMERICA, in GENERAL CONGRESS, Affembled, appealing to the Supreme Judge of the World for the Rectitude of our Intentions, do, in the Name, and by Authority of the good People of thefe Colonies, folemnly Publifh and Declare, That thefe United Colonies are, and of Right ought to be, FREE AND INDEPENDENT STATES; that they are abfolved from all Allegiance to the Britifh Crown, and that all political Connection between them and the State of Great-Britain, is and ought to be totally diffolved; and that as FREE AND INDEPENDENT STATES, they have full Power to levy War, conclude Peace, contract Alliances, eftablifh Commerce, and to do all other Acts and Things which INDEPENDENT STATES may of right do. And for the fupport of this Declaration, with a firm Reliance on the Protection of divine Providence, we mutually pledge to each other our Lives, our Fortunes, and our facred Honor.

Signed by ORDER *and in* BEHALF *of the* CONGRESS,

JOHN HANCOCK, President.

ATTEST.
CHARLES THOMSON, Secretary.

PHILADELPHIA: PRINTED BY JOHN DUNLAP.

In Congress, July 4, 1776. A Declaration by the Representatives of the United States of America..., **Philadelphia, [July 4 or 5,] 1776.**

(Pierpont Morgan Library: PML 77158)

The world learned of American independence from this celebrated broadside—the first printing of the Declaration of Independence. General Washington ordered the Declaration read to every unit in the army.

Island, the great news came from Philadelphia. Congress had voted independence. Washington ordered the Declaration of Independence read to every unit in the army "with an audible voice." The preamble proclaimed it a self-evident truth "that all men are created equal," but the proposition that Washington's soldiers were now to argue with their lives was contained in the final paragraph: "That these United Colonies are, and of Right ought to be Free and Independent States; that they are Absolved from all Allegiance to the British Crown, and that all political connection between them and the State of Great Britain, is and ought to be totally dissolved."

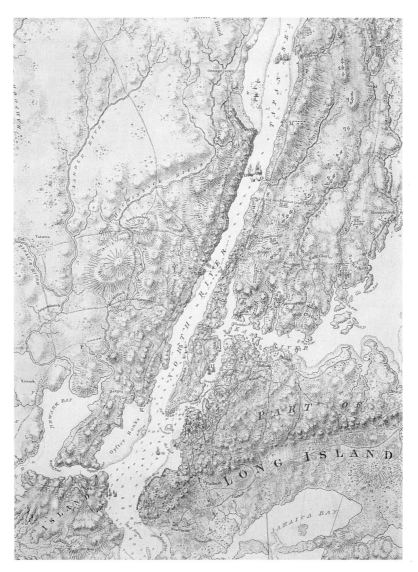

A Sketch of the Operations of His Majesty's Fleet and Army... in 1776, **London, January 17, 1777.**

(Huntington Library: Museum Map Store Collection, 93/111)

Washington's decision to defend the island city of New York put him at the mercy of a superior enemy who possessed complete command of the seas. The series of defeats that followed brought the American Revolution to the brink of ruin.

George Washington, letter signed to James Clinton, June 29 (with postscript dated July 1), 1776.

(Pierpont Morgan Library: MA 507) The British dispatched the most powerful expeditionary force in their nation's history to crush the rebellion in America. In the postscript to this letter, Washington reported the arrival of most of that force—"130 Sail" of warships and transports outside New York harbor.

More than seven years would pass before Great Britain accepted American independence. London had already deployed against the rebels the most powerful expeditionary force that England had ever sent overseas. Admiral Howe's warships, crammed with General Howe's thirty-two thousand soldiers, sailed into New York harbor even as Congress was voting independence. Howe commanded a professional army of British regulars strengthened by Hessian mercenaries that King George had hired from the German princelings. To oppose them, Washington could muster only about nineteen thousand raw volunteers. Thousands of them were not fit for duty. (Though this force was weak, it was, unfortunately for Washington, the largest body of American soldiers that he would command during the Revolution.)

Washington's experiences in the French and Indian War had taught him that militiamen could not wage sustained war. Nor could militia hope to defeat regulars in a conventional battle.

American successes gained by fighting from behind cover, like those outside Boston in 1775, were not likely to be repeated. Yet Washington decided to defend New York. He had not forgotten the lessons of the 1750s, but he may have believed that the Revolution would collapse in despair unless his army opposed the invasion. Washington's strategic misjudgment in 1776 was compounded by poor tactical planning and by his persistent expectation of better performance than his untrained soldiers could deliver on the battlefield.

The British were supremely confident. In August 1776, after weeks of leisurely preparation, Howe attacked Washington's lines on Brooklyn Heights. The Continentals crumbled like the deluded rabble the English had always known them to be. Washington did manage to bring most of the army over the river to Manhattan under cover of darkness. The battle of Long Island was the first of a string of defeats that brought the Revolution to the brink of ruin. Perhaps only the Howes' fondness for America saved Washington from destruction in 1776. The British commanders lacked the killing impulse; they may have still hoped for a political settlement.

The enemy invaded Manhattan in September. With the thunder of a spectacular naval bombardment still ringing in their ears, the redcoats came ashore from the East River, north of the little city at the southern tip of the island. They formed up and presently the well-ordered British columns started for the American trenches, advancing steadily across farmers' fields, where today the towers of Midtown grow. Washington's men sprang up from behind their earthen walls and ran in panic.

Admiral Howe's secretary watched from the flagship and recorded the British victory in his diary: "The Spirit and Activity of the Troops & Seaman were unequalled: Every man pressed to be foremost.... The dastardly Behaviour of the Rebels, on the other Hand; sinks below Remark." The "Poltroons" fled without firing a shot. General Washington would not have argued with

the Englishman's assessment of his men's performance. He tried to halt their disgraceful retreat, cursing and striking out at the fleeing soldiers. "Good God," he cried, "have I got such troops as these?" Dazed by humiliation, Washington might have been killed or captured by the advancing redcoats if aides had not pulled him off the field. Howe marched triumphantly into the city. The enemy would hold New York until the end of 1783.

American prospects darkened as autumn gave way to winter. The British chased Washington off Manhattan, up to White Plains, then over the Hudson River and south across the whole of New Jersey. All the while, the Continental Army was melting away. The enemy had captured, killed, and wounded thousands; disease, desertion, and expiring enlistments had subtracted even

François X. Habermann, *Representation du Feu terrible a Nouvelle Yorck...*, September 19, 1776, Augsburg [c. 1778].
(Huntington Library: 88539)
The Americans lost New York City when British regulars routed Washington's novices at the battle of Manhattan. A few days later, the victors lost much of their prize when the city was swept by a great fire set by patriot arsonists.

more. By the time he retreated over the Delaware River into Pennsylvania at the end of 1776, Washington had only three thousand men left. Philadelphia itself seemed to be within Howe's grasp. Congress fled to Baltimore. Washington himself despaired that soon "the game will be pretty well up." But concern for his reputation and devotion to the glorious cause required that General Washington soldier on.

Howe suspended the campaign for the winter, sending his army into winter quarters in December. He left a chain of garrisons facing the Americans. The most advanced outpost was at Trenton, on the Delaware's Jersey shore. The town was held by three Hessian regiments, about fifteen hundred men. Washington knew that he had to move quickly to revive his country's fortunes. New Year's 1777 was approaching, and, at the stroke of midnight, most of Washington's Continentals would resume the character of civilians, free to return to their homes. Exposing his army to destruction as fearlessly as he exposed his own person to danger, Washington led twenty-four hundred soldiers across the icy Delaware on Christmas night and attacked the sleeping Hessians on the morning of December 26. Surprised and befuddled by drink, the Germans soon folded. More than a thousand men were killed or captured.

An able general named Cornwallis commanded the army that rushed out to avenge the defeat. He appreciated Washington's gamble in risking his army on the British side of the Delaware. If Cornwallis could pin the Americans against the river, the rebellion would be over. But Washington skillfully slipped away and surprised a smaller enemy force at Princeton on January 3, 1777. In the fight that followed, the commander in chief rallied his faltering troops by riding within thirty yards of the ranks of firing redcoats. When the smoke cleared, his men saw him still astride his white horse, still urging them forward. Princeton was Washington's second victory in little more than a week. The uneasy British fell back on New York.

[After Charles Willson Peale, "George Washington at the battle of Princeton," 1779.]

(Huntington Art Collections: 19:13)

General Washington saved the Revolution with his miraculous little victories at Trenton and Princeton. Charles Willson Peale's portraits and prints immortalized the confident hero as the enduring symbol of the "glorious cause" the Americans had embraced.

Back from the dead, the Continental Army marched through New Jersey again, this time as victors, and General Washington began issuing pardons to those inhabitants the British had cajoled into swearing allegiance to the Crown. Eager to adhere to the winning side, many came forward. It was a complete reversal of fortune. News of Trenton and Princeton rang miraculously in the ears of a people certain that the speedy extinction of the American cause was at hand: George Washington had saved the Revolution.

Both armies marched out of winter quarters in the spring of 1777. The Continental Army was stronger than ever, its nine thousand soldiers equipped with weapons secretly provided by France. Baffled, Howe decided that he might as well take Philadelphia. He did so in September, without much trouble but also without much advantage to the British cause. Along the way, Howe beat Washington at the battles of Brandywine and Germantown, although the Americans fought surprisingly well.

But Howe's success at Philadelphia contributed to a far more costly British failure in northern New York. Had Howe moved in strength up the Hudson River Valley, he might have been able to join another British army driving down from Canada. If such an offensive had succeeded, a north-south corridor of royal power would have split apart the colonies, isolating rebellious Massachusetts. The king and his ministers still retained considerable, if misplaced, faith in the proposition that, once the New England fanatics were suppressed, the remaining colonies would resume their allegiance to the Crown. London had good reason to believe that many colonials still supported the mother country: loyalist opposition would confound the patriots throughout the Revolution. But Howe had turned instead to Philadelphia and sent only a token force up the Hudson to help the army coming south. The Americans captured that entire British army, nearly six thousand regulars and Hessians, at Saratoga in October 1777. It was an enormous victory, to be surpassed only by the triumph at Yorktown in 1781.

The fighting season for the Continental Army under

Washington's command ended with the battle of Germantown, and the two main armies retired again into winter quarters. Howe's officers and men found warm lodgings in Philadelphia. Washington's army had to camp outside the city in the barren hills of Valley Forge. The suffering of the Continental Army at Valley Forge in the winter of 1777–78 is more than legend. About one man out of every four died of hunger, disease, or exposure. Their commander was anguished by the sight of "Men, without Clothes to cover their nakedness; without Blankets to lay on; without Shoes, by which their marches might be traced, by the Blood from their Feet."

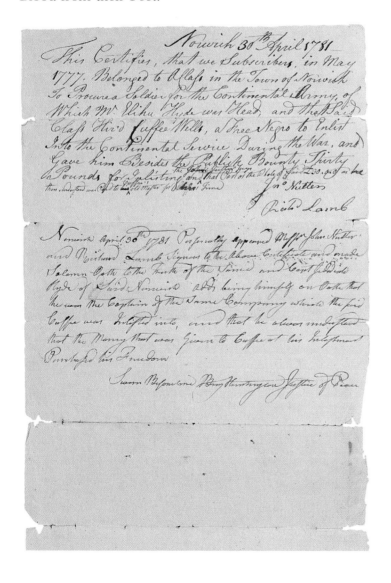

Benjamin Huntington, autograph manuscript, April 30, 1781.

(Gilder Lehrman Collection, on deposit at the Pierpont Morgan Library: GLC00318)

This affidavit documents the enlistment of an African American soldier—"Cuffee Wells, a Free Negro"—in the Continental Army. As many as one out of every seven soldiers in the American army was an African American. The black soldiers' bravery forced the Virginia slaveholder who commanded them to reconsider the familiar notions he had grown up with.

But while American soldiers perished at Valley Forge, American negotiators in Paris achieved a signal diplomatic triumph. After three years of watching, France threw its might into the struggle, tipping the balance against Great Britain. French statesmen had been encouraged by the Declaration of Independence, the victory at Saratoga, and reports of capable fighting by Washington's Continentals. They also had confidence in Washington himself, whose heroic reputation had reached across the ocean. Early in 1778, in two treaties signed at Paris, England's old adversary promised to support the Americans and, if war broke out between Britain and France, not to stop fighting until America had won its independence. Hostilities soon broke out between the two European powers. Britain now faced an enemy with a formidable navy and a war that would be waged in Europe and the Caribbean, as well as in North America. When news of the French alliance reached Valley Forge in May 1778, Washington declared a day of thanksgiving. Every man in the army welcomed a shot of rum and a chance to fire his musket in a grand salute.

Lieutenant General Sir William Howe relinquished command to Lieutenant General Sir Henry Clinton in May 1778. Clinton evacuated Philadelphia a month later. Capturing the biggest city on the continent and chasing Congress from its capital had not yielded advantages commensurate with European expectations. Indeed, the English had now occupied the three largest American cities with little profit to their cause. To prevail, the British had to take Washington's army, not cities. The American commander understood that better than his enemies. As Clinton marched his army across New Jersey to rejoin the British garrison in New York City, the Continental Army struck at the strung-out British columns. But Washington's near-victory at Monmouth Court House was wrecked by the incompetence of a subordinate general. Monmouth turned out to be the last major battle in the north. The British completed their withdrawal to New York City. Washington and his army settled down to wait outside the city. It was to be a long wait—more than three years passed before Washington challenged the enemy again in a sizable engagement. But waiting, after all, favored the rebels, not the king.

The armies were back where they had started in 1776. In the two years since the antagonists had first concentrated at New York, the portion of the Continental Army under Washington's direct command had fought eight significant battles. He had won only the two surprise attacks on Trenton and Princeton—hardly more than skirmishes by European standards. British professionals had beaten Washington at Long Island, Manhattan, White Plains, Brandywine, and Germantown. Monmouth was probably a draw.

It may not seem at first glance a record likely to enroll Washington's name among the great commanders of history. Yet it was in just such terms that the American chief was now being praised. "The old Generals of this martial Country," Benjamin Franklin reported from Paris, "join in giving you the Character of one of the greatest Captains of the Age." For the tally of battles lost and won greatly understates George Washington's achievement. He had kept his army and the cause alive. By so doing, he had won the war, even though the celebration of independence was five years away.

Washington's army was the soul of the Revolution. The Continental Congress remained little more than a provisional committee until the Articles of Confederation, adopted in 1777, were finally ratified in 1781. As presidents of Congress came and went, as Congress itself dodged from one temporary capital to another, General Washington was more a head of state than any figure in America. He struggled to maintain a coalition, not only the alliance with France, but the alliance among the thirteen states themselves. To succeed in such a command required a statesman of genius.

Washington had seen in the 1750s the destruction wrought by stubbornly disunited colonies striving to wage a common war. He had become an American nationalist before there was an

American nation. From the day of his appointment as commander in chief he had labored "to discourage all kinds of local attachments, and distinctions of Country, denominating the whole under the greater name of American." He soon became the symbol of national unity, as well as its advocate. The Revolution was fought in the name of noble ideals, but abstract principles do not always provide the most inspiring standard for rallying a people. Noble words must be made flesh, and that substance Washington provided. A few republicans feared his immense popularity, but this general did not hunger for power. Indeed, his devotion to republican principles, particularly the scrupulous obedience he gave to popular government, was the quality of Washington's leadership that his contemporaries found most heroic. As a French general wonderingly observed in 1782, "This is the seventh year that he has commanded the army, and that he has obeyed the Congress; more need not be said."

Flintlock horse pistol, one of a pair owned by George Washington, with "G. W." monogram, London.

(Mount Vernon Ladies' Association)

The Great Man:
Yorktown, Newburgh, and Annapolis

———◆•◆•◆———

*F*OR THE MOMENT the guns fell silent at Monmouth in June 1778 until the summer of 1781, the two main armies in the north remained locked in a dreary stalemate. Clinton's army garrisoned in New York; Washington's Continentals camped uncomfortably outside the city. British naval superiority gave Washington little hope of invading the island of Manhattan. Clinton did not care to venture far beyond the reach of the big guns of the Royal Navy's ships. So the two commanders dueled for control of the Hudson River. British seizure of the great waterway could still yield the potent advantage of isolating New England. But Clinton's halfhearted attacks on American posts along the river came to nothing. Benedict Arnold's betrayal of the vital American fortress at West Point in 1780 miscarried when the traitor was detected on the eve of his treachery. The deadlock in the north persisted.

But Clinton's inactivity did not spell the end of Washington's perils. At times, the Revolution seemed in danger of collapsing on itself. The states were not contributing to the war effort,

George Washington, autograph letter to John Laurens, January 30, 1781.

(Huntington Library: HM 5391)

The Revolution dragged on for more than eight years. American soldiers endured hardships that pushed some of them into rebellion. Washington put down this mutiny in January 1781. First loyal troops disarmed the mutineers. Then the rebels were forced to shoot down two of their own leaders. This broke the uprising. Washington reported without a trace of irony that "two of the principal Actors were immediately executed on the Spot, and the remainder exhibiting genuine signs of contrition, were pardoned."

and Congress had no effective way of raising money. Continental currency had depreciated so much that Washington complained that it took a wagon full of money to buy a wagonload of provisions. Hoarders and speculators grew rich while the army suffered. Washington's soldiers were unpaid, hungry, lacked decent uniforms and shoes, and were battered by the coldest winter in living memory. Their enlistments were extended without their consent. Some American soldiers were on the edge of revolt, and a few units crossed the line. Washington harshly put down several mutinies by desperate private soldiers. Men were shot down by firing squad.

Meanwhile, British strategy had shifted again: London looked south. Recognizing that the conquest of New England and the mid-Atlantic was probably no longer possible, King George and his ministry resolved to hold on to what remained of their empire south of the Potomac River. The war moved first to the Carolinas and Georgia, where English armies scored a string of impressive victories. They invaded Georgia; captured Savannah; forced the surrender of Charleston, South Carolina, and its five thousand defenders; and crushed another army at Camden, South Carolina. Lieutenant General Charles, Earl Cornwallis, commanded British forces in the south.

In 1781, Lord Cornwallis invaded Virginia. Washington followed with alarm the enemy's steady progress through his native state. But he still hoped above all for a concerted attack by the allied armies, supported by the French fleet, on Clinton in New York City. New York, however, was strongly held. The French had little faith in Washington's plan.

Fortunately for the allies, the English seemed bewildered. Perhaps Cornwallis's army should be reinforced? Perhaps the Virginia campaign should be abandoned altogether and Cornwallis evacuated by sea? Perhaps part of Cornwallis's army should sail to New York to reinforce Clinton? All of the competing plans shared one element: the need for a deep-water base on

Chesapeake Bay. Cornwallis occupied Yorktown, a little port on the peninsula formed by the York and James Rivers. His Lordship was now in a tight spot. Surrounded on three sides by water, his whole army could be fatally bottled up on the narrow neck of land. Safety depended on British naval superiority.

The allied armies were preparing to attack New York in August when news came that a powerful French fleet was on its way from the West Indies to the Chesapeake. George Washington saw at once that the distant warships might be bringing what he had longed for since 1775—the chance to land a crushing blow. He ordered an immediate march on Virginia.

For six years the commander of the Continental Army had waged a war for which he was temperamentally unsuited. Washington was an aggressive gambler. He yearned for the glory that a decisive victory could bring. He knew that only victory would return him to his beloved Mount Vernon. But the shocking defeats at New York in 1776 had taught him the lessons that would allow him to win the war. Both the imperfect instrument he wielded in the Continental Army and his deference to Congress required that Washington pursue a conservative strategy calculated to keep the army intact. Although he sometimes struck out boldly, Washington had fought a defensive war. He displayed extraordinary self-control by allowing his combative, fearless nature to be governed by prudence and his devotion to republican ideals.

British inertia contributed not a little to the triumph at Yorktown, but the two allied armies, the French navy, and the commander in chief performed brilliantly. Washington directed the logistical feat of rapidly moving seven thousand men from New York to Williamsburg, just up the peninsula from Yorktown. The French fleet had already sailed into the York River. When the Royal Navy squadron sent to break the siege was beaten off at the battle of the Chesapeake Capes on September 5, Cornwallis was doomed.

te 74   6 Dhuheim 98   Chatam 56   6 Deilleyle 64   Jnvinible 74

Le L'èle 74   Le Sangue Doc 80   L'henculle 74   Le magnanimus 74   Le Sipion 74   Le Ceptre 74

Pierre Joseph Jeunot, [view of the battle of the Chesapeake Capes].

(Huntington Library: HM 578)

In this sketch—perhaps the only depiction of the battle of the Chesapeake Capes by a participant—a young French naval officer carefully recorded the opposing lines of battle that clashed on September 5, 1781. When the Royal Navy failed to break the French blockade, Cornwallis's army at Yorktown was doomed.

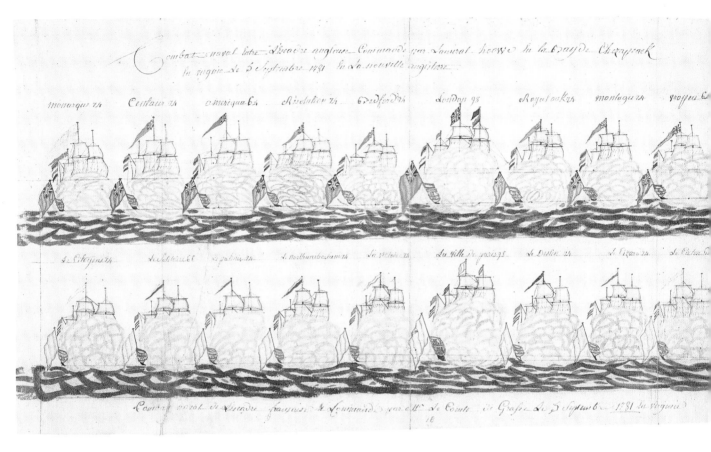

Combat naval entre l'Escadre anglaise Commandée par l'amiral hoow en la Bay de Chesapeack la virginie le 5 Septembre 1781 en La nouvelle angloise

monarque 74   Centaur 74   amerique 64   Résolution 74   Bedford 74   London 98   Royaloak 74   montagu 74   terrible 74

Le Citoyen 74   La Pallitieu 64   la galieux 74   Le northumberland 74   La vestale 74   La Ville de paris 98   Le Diadem 74   Le Cézar 74   Le Pluton 64

Combat naval de l'Escadre françoise de Commande par Mr. Le Comte De Grasse Le 5 Septemb. 1781 la virginie

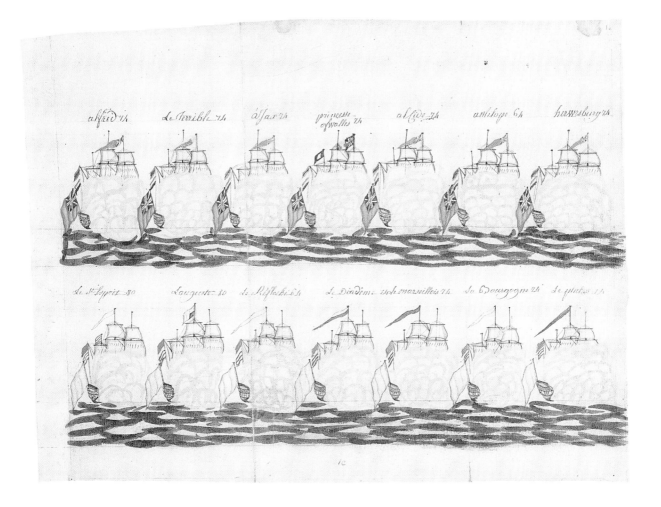

alfred 74   Le Terrible 74   ajax 74   princesse   alcide 74   antilope 64   harwesbury 74
                                          ofwalles 74

le St Esprit 80   L'auguste 80   le Reflechi 64   Le Diademe   le marsellois 74   Le Bourgogne 74   Le pluton 74

York, Virginia 17th Octr. 1781

Sir

I propose a Cessation of Hostilities for Twenty four hours, and that two Officers may be appointed by each side to meet at Mr. Moore's house to settle terms for the surrender of the posts of York & Gloucester. I have the honour to be

Sir

Your most obedient & most humble servant

Cornwallis

His Excellency General Washington &c. &c. &c.

Charles, Earl Cornwallis, letter signed to George Washington, October 17, 1781.

(Pierpont Morgan Library: MA 488)

A humiliated Cornwallis asked Washington for a twenty-four-hour truce to arrange the surrender of the British army at Yorktown. The American commander gave him just two hours to ask for terms.

By October 17, 1781, Lord Cornwallis, squirming with "mortification," had no choice but to write Washington. "I propose a Cessation of Hostilities for Twenty four hours…to settle terms for the surrender." Two days later, His Lordship found himself too indisposed to attend the ceremony. He sent a subordinate in his place. When that officer tried to present Cornwallis's sword to the commander in chief, Washington waved him aside, directing the British brigadier to make the surrender to the American second in command. Then the army of eight thousand marched out and grounded weapons. "Oh God! It is all over!" groaned the English prime minister when the news reached London. Indeed it was. Though the Continental Army would remain in the field two more years, the military phase of American Revolution had ended.

But Washington's troubles were still not over. Peace negotiations dragged on in Paris while the unpaid Continental Army waited in camp at Newburgh, New York. A long war for short rewards had at length brought the American officer corps to a state of near-rebellion. Private soldiers had mutinied before, but the general had always had his officers on his side. By late 1782 it was the officers themselves who threatened civilian authority. A

George Washington, autograph letter to James McHenry, October 17, 1782.

(Huntington Library: MH 128)

Exactly one year after Cornwallis surrendered, General Washington expressed his fear that the American army might turn against its own government: "The patience—the fortitude—the long, & great sufferings of this Army is unexampled in history; but there is an end to all things, & I fear we are very near one to this."

Newburgh 12th March 1783

Dear Sir,

I have received your letter
of the 27th Ult°, & thank you for the information
& freedom of your communication. — My offi
cial letter to Congress of this date will inform
you what has happened in this Quarter. — In
addition to which, it may be necessary it sh.d
be known to you, & to such others as you may
think proper, that the temper of the Army, tho'
very irritable on acct. of their long protracted
sufferings, has been apparently extremely
quiet while their business was depending
before Congress, until four days past. — in
the mean time it should seem, reports have
been propagated in Philadelphia that dan
gerous combinations were forming in the
Army, & this at a time when there was not
a syllable of the kind in agitation in Camp.
    It also appears that upon the arri-
val of a certain Gentleman from Philadelphia
in Camp, whose name I do not at present
incline to mention, such sentiments as these
were immediately & industriously circula
ted. —————— That it was universally ex
pected that the Army would not disband
until they had obtained Justice. ————
That the public creditors looked up to them
for redress of their grievances, would afford
them every aid, and even join them in the
field if necessary. ————— That some mem
bers of Congress wished the measure might
take effect, in order to compel the public-
particularly the delinquent States, to do
                                            Justice

foreign-born Continental colonel had already advised Washington to overthrow Congress and set himself up as king. Washington had angrily rebuked the thickheaded officer. The Americans had not been fighting for monarchy. It was as certain that Washington would have refused a kingly crown as it was certain that the people would never have offered him one.

But military revolt might have been an outcome more plausible than the crowning of an American king. The officers insisted that they would have their back pay and their promised pensions. The army could march on Philadelphia to threaten Congress, which, the officers might argue, had betrayed the republican ideals of virtuous patriotism that had guided the Revolution. If the American army had turned against its government, the result would hardly have been surprising. Popular revolutions that end in military dictatorship are not unknown to history. The prospect was certainly credible enough to horrify George Washington. He wrote that "the patience, the fortitude, the long and great sufferings of this Army is unexampled in History; but there is an end to all things, and I fear we are very near one to this."

The plotting actually began in Philadelphia. Certain politicians eager to promote stronger national government were conspiring with the discontented officers. The threat of military revolt might succeed in frightening the states into paying taxes and giving Congress new powers. This was an exceedingly dangerous game. "The army have swords in their hands," one statesman wrote another. "You know enough of the history of mankind to know much more than I have said."

The conspirators intended to use the army to reform civil government, not overthrow it. And it is unlikely in any case that an unlawful military regime could have ruled the huge territory and diverse population of the thirteen loosely confederated American states. But civil war might have been the result. Such an attempt might have made Americans too fearful of strong government to ever embrace the bold federal experiment represented by

George Washington, autograph letter to Joseph Jones, March 12, 1783.

(Huntington Library: HM 5262)
By 1783, General Washington and his army had won the war against Britain. But the outcome of the American Revolution was still in doubt. A revolution fought for noble ideals might descend into anarchy or dictatorship if the Continental Army's dissatisfied officers turned against civilian government. In this letter Washington warned Congressman Jones that seditious papers had urged the officers to threaten Congress if their demands for back pay and pensions were not met.

Cantonements 16 March 1783

Agreable to the General Orders of the 11.th Instant, The Officers of the American Army being Convend, His Excellency the Commander in Chief was pleased to Open the Meeting With the following Address to them, On the Subject of their being Called Together—

To the Gen.l Fields & Other Officers Assembled at the New Building
Pursuant to the Gen.l Orders of the 11.th Instant. March—

Gentlemen

By An Anonymous Summons, An Attempt has been Made, to Convene You Together — How Inconsistent with the Rules of Propriety; How Unmillitary — and how Subversive of all Order and Discipline — let the Good Sence of the Army Decide —

In the Moment of this Summons, Another Anonymous Production was Sent Into Circulation; Addressed More to the Feelings, and Passions, than to the Reason and Judgment of the Army — The Author of the Piece is Entitled to Much Credit for the Goodness of his Pen — and I Could Wish he had as Much Credit for the Rectitude of his heart, For, as Men See through Different Opticks, and are Induced by the Reflective Faculties of the Mind, to Use Different Means to Attain the Same end — The Author of the Address, Should have had More Charity, than to Mark for Suspicion, the Man who Should Recommend Moderation, and longer Forbearance — Or in Other Words, who Should Not think as he thinks, and Act as he Advises — But he had Another Plan in View, In which Candour and Liberallity of Sentiment, Regard to Justice, and love of Country, have No Part; and he was Right to Insinuate the darkest Suspicion to Effect the Blackest Designs —

That the Address is drawn with great Art, and is Designed to Answer the Most Insiduous Purporses — That is Calculated to Impress the Mind With An Idea of Premeditated Injustice in the Sovereign Power of the United States, and Rouse all those Resentments which Must Un-avoidably flow from Such a belief — That the Secret Mover of this Scheme (Whoever he may be Intended to take Advantage of the Passions, While they where warmd by the Recollection of Past Distreses, without giving time, for Cool, Deliberative thinking, and that Composure of mind, Which is So Necessary to give Dignity and Ability to Measures, is Rendered too Obvious, by the Mode of Conducting the Business, to Need Other Proof than A Reference to the Proceeding —

Thus Much Gentleman, I have thought it Incumbant on Me to Observe to You, to Shew upon what Principle, I Opposed the Irregular, and hasty Meeting, which was Proposed to have been held on Tuesday last; and Not because I wanted a Disposition to give you every Opportunity Consistent with your Own Honor and the Dignity of the Army, to Make Known your Grievances — If My Conduct heretofore, has not Evinced to you, that I have been A Faithfull Friend to the Army, My Declaration at this time, Would be Equally Unavailing and Improper — But as I was Among the first Who Embarked, In the Cause of Our Common Country — as I have Never left your Side One moment

the Constitution of 1787. George Washington, who had rejected suggestions that he take a leading role in the plot, believed that his officers were "wavering on a tremendous precipice" above a "gulph of Civil horror" that threatened to "deluge our rising Empire in Blood."

The Continental Army had passed another hard winter at Newburgh. In March 1783, papers written by an anonymous "fellow officer" circulated at the encampment. The author argued that the officers must never lay down their arms until they had wrested from their ungrateful country the justice their years of sacrifice had earned. He called for a mutinous mass meeting of the officer corps. Washington countered by calling an official meeting in the officers' assembly hall, known as the Temple of Virtue.

Washington used his twenty-minute speech and a bit of inspired stagecraft to remind the skeptical and even hostile officers of the true meaning of their Revolution. The Continental Army had fought not only to preserve American liberties from a perceived threat of tyranny. They also had fought to create a republican society, and a republic's vital spark was the virtue of its people. The survival of a republic required that those citizens with ambition and talent sacrifice their own interests to the greater good of their country. This the army had done for eight years. For the officers to repudiate their selflessness in the final passage of the great struggle would betray virtue and tarnish the glorious fame that promised to ennoble them to posterity. Washington pleaded with his officers to demonstrate political heroism that would match their battlefield courage. Congress would do them justice, he vowed. They must be patient a little longer.

However convincing the speech may have been, the emblematic flourish that followed won the day for Washington. He began to read a letter from a congressman. But something was wrong. His Excellency faltered, was unable to read, and finally drew from his pocket a pair of spectacles. None of the officers had ever seen him wear them. Placing the glasses on his face, Washington said,

George Washington, manuscript address ("To the Genls., Fields, & Other Officers Assembled"), March [15,] 1783.

(Huntington Library: HM 1607) Washington's quelling of a threatened mutiny by the Continental Army's angry officers may have saved America from military despotism. In this dramatic speech General Washington pleaded with his officers to exhibit political heroism to match their battlefield courage. Washington won over the rebellious officers— and saved the American Revolution.

George III, autograph letter to Thomas Townshend, November 19, 1782.

(Huntington Library: HM 25755) Among the last Britons to accept defeat was King George III—the stubborn man who had once declared that "blows must decide." In this historic letter the king finally bowed to the inevitable, instructing a diplomat to go ahead with the treaty that will establish American independence. Still unable to stomach the word, His Majesty has crossed out "Independence" in the phrase "granting Independence to North America" and substituted "a Seperation."

"Gentlemen, you must pardon me. I have grown gray in the service of my country and now find myself going blind." He finished the letter and left the hall without another word. The gesture, conveying both Washington's humanity and his dedication to the cause, pierced the hearts of his men. Many a once-rebellious officer was moved to tears. They immediately declared their loyalty to civilian government. George Washington had saved the Revolution again.

Three days later, on March 18, 1783, word reached Newburgh that peace had been concluded in Paris: Great Britain had at last recognized the independence of the United States. Negotiations had begun in earnest in September 1782, almost a year after Yorktown. By November, even the obstinate King George was ready to give up. In a letter precisely dated "Windsor Nov. 19th. 1782 23 min[utes] p[as]t 10 PM," His Royal Highness directed the home secretary to go ahead with the treaty. But only,

Mrs. General Washington, Bestowing thirteen Stripes on Britania.

"Mrs: General Washington Bestowing thirteen Stripes on Britannia," in *The Rambler's Magazine... for March 1783*, London, 1783.

(Huntington Library: 478018)

This cartoon appeared in the racy London magazine *The Rambler* with a tongue-in-cheek report that the American commander was actually a woman. Perhaps satirically emasculating the victor helped to take some of the sting out of the terrible geopolitical thrashing that Britannia had suffered when defeat wrested away the choicest part of the empire.

the king lamented, because "Parliament having to my astonishment come into the ideas of granting ~~Independence~~ a Seperation to North America, has disabled Me from longer defending the just rights of this Kingdom." The treaty was signed ten days later.

All that remained was for the principal actor to make his exit, and this he did with the greatest care. Washington first drafted a farewell address in the form of a letter to the governors of the states. Here he advanced certain propositions: The United States could become a great and powerful and happy nation. By its example America could lead the world into a new era of freedom. Like Tom Paine, George Washington was suggesting that the American experiment could recast the future. "With our fate will the destiny of unborn Millions be involved."

But the experiment could as easily fail. Washington insisted that a vigorous national government—"An indissoluble Union of the States under one Federal Head"—was "essential to the well being, I may even venture to say, to the existence of the United States as an Independent Power." His ideas carried a greater moral authority since they were those of a man leaving the stage of public life forever. He could pledge that "no sinister views" influenced him—if a stronger government were created, George Washington would take no part and would gain no high office.

General Washington triumphantly entered New York the day the British evacuated the city. He soon left for Annapolis, then the seat of Congress. There, on December 23, 1783, Washington ceremoniously handed back to the president of Congress the parchment commission that he had received in Philadelphia on June 15, 1775. Since then, Congress had seen eight presidents, the Continental Army a single commander. Washington made a brief farewell address, resigning "with satisfaction the Appointment I accepted with diffidence," and taking his "leave of all the employments of public life." He mounted his horse and rode hard to reach Mount Vernon on Christmas Eve, 1783.

Giving up power was more glorious than winning the war. By stepping down, Washington had raised himself up to a pinnacle of fame as the embodiment of republican heroism. According to one story, George III asked the American painter Benjamin West what General Washington was likely to do when peace came. Would he stay with the army? Would he become head of state? West replied that Washington would probably return to his farm. The king was astounded. If Washington does that, His Majesty declared, he will be the greatest man in the world. The story may be apocryphal, but most Americans and not a few Europeans now considered George Washington the most distinguished figure of the age.

First Citizen

MERICA'S FIRST CITIZEN returned home after an eight-year absence to find his private affairs in disarray. Mount Vernon was run down. A renovation of the mansion house that Washington had begun a full decade earlier remained unfinished. The roof leaked. The farms were unproductive. Eighteen Mount Vernon slaves had escaped to seek freedom with the British. Many debtors had paid Washington in vastly depreciated Continental currency; others had not bothered to pay at all. The republican commander, who had refused any salary for his military service, promptly submitted his wartime expense account for reimbursement. It came to $64,335.30, or about $7,500 a year. But the government paid him off in devalued certificates, some of which he was forced to sell at one-twentieth of their face value. Family and friends soon came with their hands out. Washington had to tell them that he had no cash to spare.

In spite of it all, he was overjoyed to be home. "I feel now,"

Washington, autograph document ("The United States in Account with G: Washington"), December 13–28, 1783.

(Huntington Library: HM 5502) These entries record Washington's expenses during the last few days of his eight and one-half years as commander of the Continental Army. Republican virtue had prompted Washington to refuse any salary for his service. He asked only that his expenses be met. The total came to $64,335.30—about $7500 a year. Congress paid him off in depreciated Continental currency.

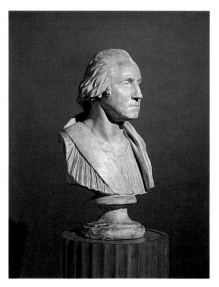 

Jean-Antoine Houdon, "George Washington," plaster bust, 1787.

(Dr. Gary Milan)

The great sculptor crossed the Atlantic in 1785 to capture the fifty-three-year-old hero at the pinnacle of his fame in this, probably the finest portrait of George Washington ever achieved.

Washington wrote one of his generals, as "a wearied Traveller must do, who, after treading many a painful step, with a heavy burden on his shoulders, is eased of the latter, having reached the Goal to which all the former were directed, and from his House top is looking back, and tracing with a grateful eye the Meanders by which he has escaped the quicksands and Mires which lay in his way."

Cash-poor though he may have been, George Washington was still a mighty rich man. Most considerable of his assets was his western land. Although the native inhabitants had not been consulted, the 1783 treaty had established that the Ohio Valley—the Northwest Territory—was U.S. soil. Washington's particular concerns were his tracts on the Ohio, which embraced, he calculated, some thirty-three thousand acres. "There is no richer, or more valuable land in all that Region," he boasted. But the land's promise was overshadowed by the lack of a practical means to bring its produce to market. Moving bulk goods overland would never pay. The long trip down the Mississippi to Spanish New Orleans was strewn with dangers. Washington saw a growing threat not only to his private fortune but to the integrity of the new nation itself. He believed that without an

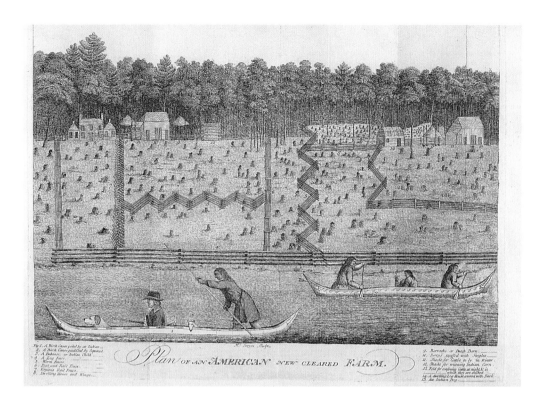

Plan OF AN AMERICAN NEW CLEARED FARM.

alliance of mutual interest based on trade the Ohio Valley settlers might align themselves with Spain or Britain.

Washington soon revived his scheme to build a canal and
road system linking the Potomac and Ohio. He was named president of the Potomac Navigation Company, duly chartered by
Virginia and Maryland. Such a mammoth engineering project
required cooperation between the states, but little such cooperation was evident. Under the Articles of Confederation the states
had consented to join only in a "firm league of friendship" in
which each state retained "its sovereignty, freedom and independence." Americans had always feared centralized power, and so
by design, the Articles furnished a feeble central government.

George Washington and other nationalists, imbued with a
"continental vision" by their experiences in the Revolution, were
convinced that the republican experiment would fail unless popular government was supported by a firm union of the states. "I
can foresee no evil greater, than disunion," Washington wrote in

"Plan of an American New Cleared Farm," in Patrick Campbell, *Travels in . . . North America in the Years 1791 and 1792,* Edinburgh, 1793.
(Huntington Library: 18609)
After the Revolution, pio-
neers poured into the frontier lands of the west, carv-
ing out farms and adding
new states to the union.
George Washington had
promoted the development
of the west for fifty years. As
private citizen, and later as
president, Washington did all
he could to encourage the
settlement of Indian lands.

"General Washington's Jack Ass," in *Weatherwise's Town and Country Almanack for...* **1786, Boston, [1785].**

(Huntington Library: 424665)

Washington's most successful agricultural innovation was his introduction of the mule to America. The king of Spain presented Washington with a rare Andalusian Jack Ass. Washington bred the valuable animal with mares to establish what he called an "excellent race of mules." This woodcut of the Jack Ass appeared over a few lines of republican doggerel that concluded "Asses, Kings, Ministers are all one blood."

August 1785. Without an effective national government, he was certain that America "never shall establish a National character, or be considered on a respectable footing by the Powers of Europe.... We are either a United people under one head, & for Federal purposes, or, we are thirteen independent Sovereignties, eternally counteracting each other." Foreign powers continued to treat the United States with the contempt its impotence invited. The Confederation was as weak at home, unable to collect taxes, pay down the war debt, and regulate trade.

But certain outbursts of popular discontent were more

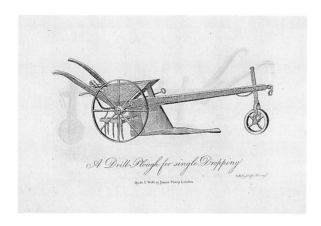

A Drill Plough for single Dropping
Made & Sold by James Sharp London.

[George Washington's copy], *Descriptions of some of the Utensils in Husbandry . . . &C. Made and Sold by James Sharp*, London, [c. 1785].
(Pierpont Morgan Library: unaccessioned books)
Washington built a seed drill like this at Mount Vernon. The drill was a state-of-the-art farming machine that plowed a furrow, dropped in seeds, and covered them in a single operation. Calibrating the machine required Washington to calculate the number of grains in a bushel of Timothy seed (13,410,000).

alarming to Washington than were the frailties of the Confederation. Many feared an "excess of democracy" almost as much as they had feared British tyranny a decade earlier. As conceived by men like Washington, theirs was a revolution that would not bring revolutionary social change. The equality for which they had fought was an equality of rights, not social station. Distinctions would remain in the new, republican America. Lesser folk would still defer to the betters, and the management of public affairs would always be entrusted to gentlemen. Men of sufficient talent and ambition, whatever their birth, could enter the ranks of the gentry, but none but gentlemen should govern. History would demonstrate that Washington and many of his contemporaries were mistaken in their apprehension of the American future. Before long, egalitarianism would prevail, and the traditional society of deference would be swept away. Popular democracy would supplant classical republicanism. Common men would decide elections and hold high offices.

In the time of the Confederation, however, it seemed to many that the preservation of the culture of deference was not only possible but also necessary for the survival of republican government. Anarchy followed by despotism seemed the only alternative. So Washington was shocked in 1786 when debt-burdened Massachusetts farmers revolted in an outbreak of lawlessness, known as Shays's Rebellion. These rebels appeared to be levelers

Chinese export porcelain platter bearing the insignia of the Society of the Cincinnati.

(The Louise and Barry Taper Collection)

Washington purchased a full service of Cincinnati china in 1786. Founded in 1783, the Society of the Cincinnati was a fraternal organization of officers who had served in the American and French forces during the Revolution. Washington became cautious about his involvement with the Cincinnati after Thomas Jefferson warned him that the society's hereditary charter, suggestive of European aristocracy, threatened republican liberties.

Custine cup and saucer with GW cipher.

(The Louise and Barry Taper Collection)

This cup is from a porcelain service given to Martha Washington in 1782 by the Comte de Custine-Sarreck, owner of the Niderville factory in France and one of the French officers who fought with Washington in the Revolution.

intent on rooting out all social distinction. They threatened rights of property. It was a nightmare that Washington called a "formidable rebellion against the laws & constitutions of our own making." He dashed off an anxious letter to one of his old generals in Massachusetts: "Are your people getting mad?—Are we to have the goodly fabric that eight years were spent in rearing pulled over our heads?" Washington now feared that the entire enterprise to which he had devoted so much of his life teetered again on the brink of ruin. "Our Affairs, generally," he wrote in February 1787, "seem really, to be approaching to some awful crisis."

By 1787, however, new hope approached in the shape of the convention set to meet in Philadelphia in May. Its delegates would try "to devise such further provisions as shall appear to them necessary to render the constitution of the Federal Government adequate to the exigencies of the Union." This they were to do only by amending the Articles of Confederation. Instead, the delegates would radically exceed their instructions, scrapping the Articles and creating a strong central government under the United States Constitution. Not only could such a union establish the United States among the nations of the earth, but it also might serve to shift the political high ground from the local to the national level, undercutting the influence of supposed social revolutionaries, such as those who had emerged in Massachusetts.

Naturally, Virginia named George Washington one its delegates to the Constitutional Convention. He declined. Had he not solemnly promised the American people in 1783 that he was forever taking "leave of all the employments of public life"? Had he not achieved his most brilliant success by relinquishing power? His reputation was secure; reentering the political sphere could only put it at risk. It took months of agonizing on Washington's part, and earnest appeals from leading nationalists, to convince the great man that his presence at the convention was indispensable. Certain twentieth-century historians have taken Washington to task for his vacillation, ascribing it to an unseemly preoccupation with his honor. But chances are that George Washington understood the stakes better than the historians did.

Washington had long supported strong national government and had stated that support many times since 1775. He knew that he might be required to play a role if such a government was created. He also understood that the trust he had earned was one of the most precious assets the new nation possessed. That prestige could not be squandered on any attempt that might fail to establish a stronger government. And his ability to lead might be damaged if the people believed that he had broken his word. But

George Washington, autograph letter to John Francis Mercer, September 9, 1786.

(The Gilder Lehrman Collection, on deposit at the Pierpont Morgan Library: GLC 3705) Washington recognized that slavery violated the Revolution's ideals of liberty and equality. He also feared that slavery might divide South from North, preventing the federal union of the states he so much desired. Here he declared that "I never mean...to possess another slave by purchase; it being among my first wishes to see some plan adopted, by which slavery in this Country may be abolished by slow, sure, & imperceptible degrees."

Mount Vernon 9th. Sep 1786

Dear Sir,

Your favor of the 20th. ulto. did not reach me till about the first inst. — It found me in a fever, from which I am now but sufficiently recovered to attend to business. — I mention this to shew that I had it not in my power to give an answer to your propositions sooner. —

With respect to the first. I never mean (unless some particular circumstances should compel me to it) to possess another slave by purchase; it being among my first wishes to see some plan adopted by which slavery in this country may be abolished by slow, sure, & imperceptable degrees. — With respect to the 2d, I never did, nor never intend to purchase a military certificate; — I see no difference it makes with you (if it is one of the funds allotted for the discharge of my claim) who the the purchaser

is

Washington also recognized that his reputation might suffer if he sat out the convention while other men struggled with the "awful crisis." He feared that his "non-attendance in this Convention [would] be considered as a dereliction to republicanism." His fame could hardly be expected to light the coming ages if the revolution he had directed ended in failure. By March 1787, Washington had accepted the interruption of his happy retirement.

George Washington returned to the stage with reluctance and apprehension. His business affairs, like Mount Vernon's several thousand acres, demanded constant attention. He was the fifty-five-year-old heir of a line of men who seldom attained fifty. Age was finally overtaking him, he believed, diminishing his powers. Rheumatism prevented him from raising one arm above his shoulder. He had lost most of his teeth, a fact that surely deepened his dread of public speaking. He feared that his memory was increasingly faulty. He mistrusted his abilities as a statesman. And he must have shuddered at what the creation of a new national government promised to bring. It did not require the gift of prophecy to see that America was likely to call on him again.

Of all the issues that threatened to wreck accord among the states at the convention, none was more dangerous than slavery. On a gloomy day in February 1786, Washington had ridden across his farms counting certain of the people who lived and worked at Mount Vernon. He counted only those who were black. These people were slaves—what Washington once called a "certain species of property." A careful proprietor accounts for his property—the slaves were inventoried by age, sex, and occupation. When he had completed the task, Washington recorded the result in a pocket diary: 216 men, women, and children. A few weeks earlier he had counted his livestock, noting in the same diary the numbers of horses, cattle, sheep, and oxen that grazed Mount Vernon's fields.

But this chilling juxtaposition of two exercises in farm management does not fairly reflect Washington's growing repug-

George Washington, autograph letter to James McHenry, November 11, 1786.

(The Gilder Lehrman Collection, on deposit at the Pierpont Morgan Library: GLC 2065)

Washington hoped for the gradual abolition of slavery by legislative action. But he never publicly endorsed emancipation. And he vigorously defended slaveholders' property rights in their human assets. In this letter Washington proposed a scheme to trick a runaway slave into recapture.

nance for slavery. The lavish life that Washington and his family enjoyed had always been earned by the labor of enslaved people. Still, by 1786, Washington believed that slavery should be abolished, although he would never say so publicly. "I never mean," he wrote, "to possess another slave by purchase; it being among my first wishes to see some plan adopted, by which slavery in this Country may be abolished by slow, sure, & imperceptible degrees." About this time, Washington told a confidant that the "unfortunate condition of the persons, whose labour in part I employed, has been the only unavoidable subject of regret. To make the Adults among them as easy & as comfortable in their circumstances as their actual state of ignorance & improvidence would admit; & to lay a foundation to prepare the rising generation for a destiny different from that in which they were born;

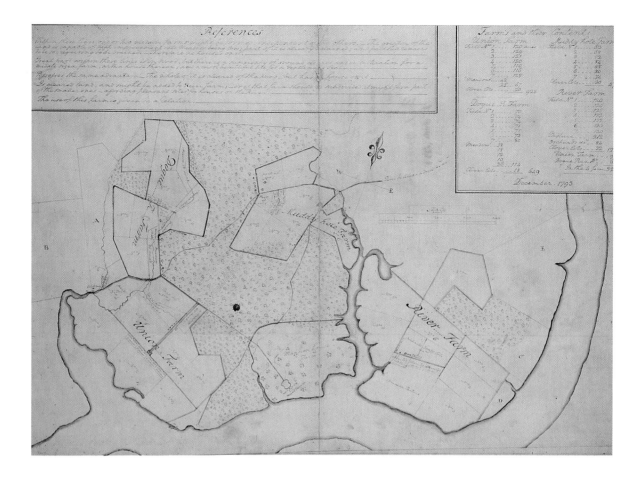

afforded some satisfaction to my mind, & could not I hoped be displeasing to the justice of the Creator."

Washington had been influenced by republican ideology and by his fear that slavery might permanently sunder South from North. The master of Mount Vernon had decided, even before the Revolution, to buy no more slaves. The shift from planting tobacco to farming grain crops had reduced the number of laborers needed to operate Mount Vernon. Still, he could not simply sell off those he did not need. "To sell the overplus I cannot," he would write near the end of his life, "because I am principled against this kind of traffic in the human species. To hire them out, is almost as bad, because they could not be disposed of in families to any advantage, and to disperse the families I have an aversion. What then is to be done?"

George Washington, autograph map of Mount Vernon, December 1793.
(Huntington Library: HM 5995. Original map not in exhibition.) Washington drafted this map of his eight-thousand-acre estate to further his plan to lease the Mount Vernon farms to tenants. Washington believed that the arrangement would allow him to free his slaves. The freed people could stay on at Mount Vernon and work as paid agricultural laborers.

(*Private*)

(✳)

> Besides these, I have another motive which makes me earnestly wish for the accomplishment of these things — it is indeed more powerful than all the rest. namely to liberate a certain species of property which I possess, very repugnantly to my own feelings; but which imperious necessity compels; & until I can substitute some other expedient, by which expences not in my power to avoid (however well disposed I may be to do it) ~~can~~ can be defrayed. —

George Washington, autograph note to an autograph letter to Tobias Lear, May 6, 1794.

(Huntington Library: HM 5229) In a confidential note to his secretary describing Washington's plan to lease the Mount Vernon farms to tenants, Washington revealed his true objective. "More powerful" than his "motive" to free himself from the burden of managing Mount Vernon was the desire to free his slaves: "to liberate a certain species of property which I possess, very repugnantly to my own feelings." Washington's plan failed because he was unable to find suitable tenants.

Mount Vernon. 7th Novr. 1786.

My dear Sir,

I have, I think, seen your name mentioned as President of the Society of the Cincinnati in the State of Massachusetts. — For this reason I give you the trouble of the enclosed address.

I hope your wishes were fully accomplished in your Eastern trip. — Are your people getting mad? — Are we to have the goodly fabrick that eight years were spent in rearing pulled over our heads? — What is the cause of all these commotions? — When & how is it to end? —

I need not repeat to you how much

I am My dear Sir
Yr most obedt & affect.
Hble Servant
G. Washington

Genl Lincoln.

George Washington, autograph letter to Benjamin Lincoln, November 7, 1786.
(The Gilder Lehrman Collection, on deposit at the Pierpont Morgan Library: GLC1479)
The uprising of Massachusetts farmers known Shays's Rebellion raised Washington's fears that an "excess of democracy" threatened to destroy the great experiment in self-government. He dashed off this letter to one of his former generals: "Are your people getting mad?—Are we to have the goodly fabric that eight years were spent in rearing pulled over our heads?" Washington and other nationalists believed that only the creation of a strong central government could head off popular anarchy.

Neither Washington nor his country ever discovered a satisfactory answer to that question. In the 1790s, while serving as president in Philadelphia, Washington attempted a reorganization of his estates that would, he hoped, allow him to set his slaves free while providing him with a steady income and the freed people with a way of making a living. He intended to lease the Mount Vernon farms to capable (and preferably English) agriculturists. The tenants would shoulder the burden of managing the eight-thousand-acre estate. But Washington's foremost objective was to disentangle himself from slavery: "I have another motive which makes me earnestly wish for the accomplishment of these things, it is indeed more powerful than all the rest. Namely to liberate a certain species of property which I possess, very repugnantly to my own feelings; but which imperious necessity compels." The sturdy English farmers would operate Mount Vernon so efficiently that the slaves could be emancipated to stay on as paid agricultural laborers. But the scheme failed when no suitable tenants appeared. In the end, Washington elected to emancipate his slaves after his death. It was a radical decision but known to the world only after his will was published.

All Washington's fears were confirmed by the debates at the Constitutional Convention: No union of the states could survive a concerted effort to restrict slavery.

George Washington, autograph letter to Henry Knox, February 25, 1787.

(The Gilder Lehrman Collection, on deposit at the Pierpont Morgan Library: 2437 LIII, 59)

Washington hoped he could avoid attending the Constitutional Convention in May 1787. "Our Affairs," he wrote a friend, "seem really, to be approaching to some awful crisis. God only knows what the result will be. It shall be my part to hope for the best; as to see this Country happy whilst I am gliding down the stream of life in tranquil retirement is so much the wish of my Soul."

"The Fate of Unborn Millions"

GEORGE WASHINGTON, it might be said, played only a small role in the creation of the U.S. Constitution. One might as easily argue that he was the principal player in the drama of the Grand Federal Convention of 1787. He took almost no part in the debates. He was largely unacquainted with theories of constitutionalism. Yet Washington's majestic presence steadied and gave legitimacy to the Constitutional Convention, the very legality of which many questioned. Later, ratification of the Constitution would probably have been impossible without Washington's support. ("Be assured," one of the Constitution's opponents would complain, "his influence carried this government.") As many historians have observed, ratification of the Constitution was a sort of ratification of George Washington himself. Certainly the powerful office of the presidency, one of the most remarkable features of the new government, was crafted to conform to the flawless character of George Washington. Everyone knew that he would be first to wield the substantial powers of the office.

The delegates (fifty-five men representing every state but

Charles Willson Peale, "A N.W. View of the State House in Philadelphia taken in 1778," in *Columbian Magazine... July 1787*, Philadelphia, 1787.

(Huntington Library: 39009)

Throughout the sultry summer of 1787, the Constitutional Convention met in secret session in the Pennsylvania State House. When the Convention convened, the delegates quickly elected George Washington its president.

Rhode Island would attend at one time or another) convened at the Pennsylvania State House, where the Continental Congress had commissioned Washington general twelve years earlier. The new assembly now elected Washington its president. It was a role he welcomed. His exalted standing was recognized, and he was exempted from speaking during debates.

The Virginia delegation dominated the meeting from the start. Washington furnished his massive grandeur, and thirty-six-year-old James Madison (deservedly remembered as the Father of the Constitution) brought political genius and encyclopedic knowledge of constitutional republics, ancient and modern. Madison's leadership assured that a well-rehearsed Virginia delegation appeared at the first session with an altogether radical proposal. On May 29, 1787, the delegation offered the fifteen resolutions known as the Virginia plan. Though George Washington did not speak, everyone understood that he supported the plan.

The resolutions mapped out a supreme national government that would derive its power from the consent of the people. It would be composed of executive, legislative, and judicial branches, like the governments of the individual states. The

Pierce Butler, autograph manuscript, May 30, 1787.

(The Gilder Lehrman Collection, on deposit at the Pierpont Morgan Library: GLC 819.04)

The delegates to the Constitutional Convention agreed on the radical proposition that a powerful federal government must be created to save the republican experiment. South Carolina delegate Pierce Butler recorded the momentous resolution in the notebook he kept at the Convention: "May the 30th. 1787. Resolved therefore that a National Government ought to be Established, Consisting of a supreme legislative, judiciary & Executive."

national government would possess sweeping powers to act directly on its citizens. Representation would be proportional, probably based on population. Although proportional representation seemed most consistent with republican principles, it departed from the one-state, one-vote formula that had prevailed since the first Congress of 1774.

The Virginia plan was radical. The call for the creation of a supreme national government was a call for a second American revolution. And no one could doubt that such a scheme went far beyond the directive of the Confederation Congress that the convention meet for the "sole and express purpose of revising the Articles of Confederation." Yet the next day, the whole convention boldly voted for a resolution "that a *national* Government ought to be established consisting of a *supreme* Legislative, Executive, and Judiciary." The delegates seemed to agree that the American experiment could be preserved only by such a revolutionary expedient.

But the treacherous question of state representation soon brought the convention to a near-fatal deadlock. The large-state nationalists and other proponents of vigorous government supported the Virginia plan and proportional representation. Many small-state delegates, along with others who feared powerful government, favored a federal union in which the central authority

Pierce Butler, autograph manuscript, [c. August 1787].

(The Gilder Lehrman Collection, on deposit at the Pierpont Morgan Library: GLC 819.23)

Many questioned whether republican government could work in a large country. Such doubts were expressed on the floor of the Constitutional Convention in 1787, as this undated note from Pierce Butler's papers shows: "It is the opinion of this Convention that the Teritory of the States is too extensive to Consist of One Republic only—Resolved therefore that…the security of equal liberty and general welfare will be best preserved and Continued by forming the States into three Republicks—distinct in their Governments."

was endowed with less sweeping powers. The real sticking point was the small states' insistence on the one-state, one-vote formula. They feared being buried by the larger states. But Madison and his allies insisted as vehemently that a republican nation founded on the bedrock principle that all people were created equal must give its citizens an equal voice. As one of the nationalists put it, one hundred fifty Pennsylvanians should not be required to equal fifty citizens of New Jersey. As the impasse dragged on, tempers inside the State House grew as heated as the summer weather outside.

The delegates could not go home without achieving something, and debate had already suggested one way out. The Virginia plan called for a national legislature composed of an upper house and a lower house. The small states would agree to popular representation in the lower house if given an equal vote in the upper. James Madison and some of the other nationalists bitterly opposed sacrificing republican principles to appease the small states. Supporters of the bargain never convinced Madison, but they did manage to outvote him. The Great Compromise of July 16 broke the deadlock and cleared the way for agreement on the other issues. The states would be equally represented in the upper house, later named the Senate. Population would determine membership in the lower body, the House of Representatives. Slaves would be reckoned as three-fifths of free inhabitants in determining population.

By the end of July, the delegates had made enough progress to call a ten-day recess while a small committee worked out a draft of a proposed constitution. Washington sought diversion. He visited Charles Willson Peale's museum and William Bartram's botanical gardens. Always happy to oblige artists, he sat patiently as the Peales, father and son, labored to translate his likeness to canvas. The flesh-and-blood Washington found fishing an amusing pastime, and he and a fellow delegate rode out to "Valley-forge to get Trout." But, he recorded in his diary, "whilst Mr. Morris was fishing I rid over the old Cantonment of the American [army] in the Winter of 1777, & 8. Visited all the Works, wch. were in Ruins."

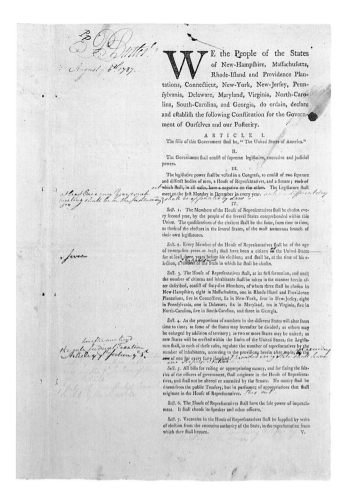

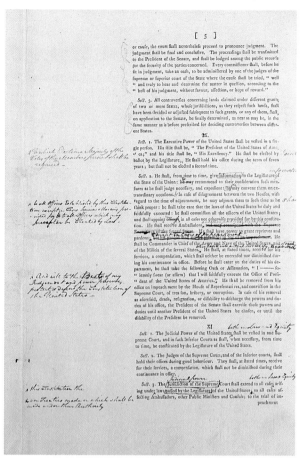

***We the People of the
States of New-Hampshire,
Massachusetts, Rhode-
Island...*, Philadelphia,
August 6, 1787, folios [1]
and 5.**

(The Gilder Lehrman Collection,
on deposit at the Pierpont Morgan
Library: GLC 819.01)

The "Report of the
Committee of Detail," the
first draft of the U.S.
Constitution, was secretly
printed—with wide margins
for notetaking—at about the
halfway point in the debates.

Only a few copies of the
"Report" survive today,
including this, Pierce
Butler's copy from the
Gilder Lehrman Collection,
as well as copies in the
Pierpont Morgan Library
and the Huntington Library.

Characteristically, Washington wrote nothing of the feelings that the scenes must have stirred in him.

When the convention met again on August 6, the result of the committee's work was distributed to the delegates. A few copies of this "Report of the Committee of Detail" had been secretly printed on seven tall folio sheets, provided with wide margins wherein members could record changes made during the debates. The report was the first draft of the U.S. Constitution. Within its articles, the lineaments of Madison's Virginia plan were clearly discernible.

Many questions about the executive remained. Suspicion of power concentrated in the hands of a single figure was a central feature of republican ideology. It would hardly have been surprising if the convention had severely restricted the powers of the office. Proposals to do just that had been floated in the debates: A committee of three might compose the executive. The president could be appointed by the legislature or the judiciary and be subject to recall. Veto power could be withheld. The states might be vested with impeachment powers. An appointed advisory council might hedge presidential autonomy. The president might not be named commander in chief of the nation's military or be accorded a major role in setting foreign policy. Service could be limited to a single term.

Instead, the convention created a single strong, independent executive officer. In his silence, Washington had shaped that decision. Pierce Butler of South Carolina thought that the president's powers were "full great, and greater than I was disposed to make them. Nor (entre nous) do I believe they would have been so great had not many of the members cast their eyes towards General Washington as President; and shaped their ideas of the Powers to be given a President, by their opinions of his Virtue."

As the gentlemen in Philadelphia charted the boundaries of the political freedom accruing to future generations of white Americans, about five hundred thousand black inhabitants of

America, nearly one-fifth of the whole population, were held in perpetual slavery. Though slavery was still legal in many of the northern states, nearly all the enslaved people lived in the South. Indeed, in many southern districts the black population equaled or exceeded the white population. The new Constitution offered nothing to these captive people or their posterity. Slavery was by far the most explosive issue the delegates faced. Both underlying and overshadowing the rivalry between big and small states, slavery had already divided the country into two antagonistic sections. Everyone knew that the South—particularly powerful South Carolina, along with North Carolina and Georgia—would never agree to a constitution that gave the federal government substantial powers over the institution of slavery. The southern states would come into the union with their slaves or not at all. They also insisted on guarantees that their hold on the enslaved would remain secure long into the future.

Few southern statesmen defended the morality of slavery in 1787, but fewer still hoped for its abolition. No one could doubt that the institution was an open and pernicious violation of the principle of human equality that had driven the American Revolution—the same principle of equality on which the convention was now constructing a republican government. But politics triumphed over ideology. The delegates chose national unity over natural rights and so postponed the day of reckoning. They

Pierce Butler, autograph manuscript (draft of the fugitive slave cause), [c. August 28, 1787].
(The Gilder Lehrman Collection, on deposit at the Pierpont Morgan Library: GLC 819.17)
The U.S. Constitution protected slavery and offered nothing to the half-million Americans held in bondage. Slaveholder Pierce Butler introduced the motion that became the fugitive slave clause of the U.S. Constitution. The provision required the free states to return escaped slaves to their masters. This draft in Butler's hand differs from the version adopted in the Constitution.

bequeathed to the unborn millions a contradictory legacy of freedom and slavery.

Whenever possible, the delegates tried to sidestep the issue altogether. The words "slave" and "slavery" appear nowhere in the Constitution. The preferred code phrases "person held to service or labor," "all other persons," and "such persons" of course puzzled no one. Most far-reaching of the concessions made to slave power was the three-fifths rule of counting population. Every new slave born or imported would increase slave state representation in Congress. The tax that federal government could impose on newly imported slaves was limited to ten dollars, and government regulation of transatlantic slave trade was forbidden for twenty years. The Constitution also included the fugitive slave clause introduced by Pierce Butler. Under this provision the supreme law of the land obliged the northern states and their citizens to return escaped slaves to bondage.

The Constitution, consisting of a preamble and seven articles, was signed by thirty-nine delegates on September 17. A glance at the first lines hinted at the summer's progress. The preamble to the first draft of early August had opened "We the People of the States of..." listing all thirteen states by name, in geographical order from north to south. The Constitution itself began "We the People of the United States." But harmony did not entirely prevail. Three influential delegates had refused to sign. And all the framers recognized that it would not be easy to persuade the states to accept the proposed charter.

The Federalists (as the Constitution's supporters called themselves) had improved their chances by providing that ratification by only nine of the thirteen states would be sufficient to establish the Union "between the States so ratifying." They had also stipulated ratification by special conventions, neatly bypassing the troublesome state legislatures, which were likely to resist surrendering authority to a new federal government.

The convention had conducted its business in strict secrecy,

WE, the People of the United States, in order to form a more perfect union, establish juſtice, inſure domeſtic tranquility, provide for the common defence, promote the general welfare, and ſecure the bleſſings of liberty to ourſelves and our poſterity, do ordain and eſtabliſh this Conſtitution for the United States of America.

ARTICLE I.

Sect. 1. ALL legiſlative powers herein granted ſhall be veſted in a Congreſs of the United States, which ſhall conſiſt of a Senate and ~~~~ of Repreſentatives.

Sect. 2. The Houſe of Repreſentatives ſhall be compoſed of members choſen every ſecond year by the people of the ſeveral ſtates, and the electors in each ſtate ſhall have the qualifications requiſite for electors of the moſt numerous branch of the ſtate legiſlature.

No perſon ſhall be a repreſentative who ſhall not have attained to the age of twenty-five years, and been ſeven years a citizen of the United States, and who ſhall not, when elected, be an inhabitant of that ſtate in which he ſhall be choſen.

Repreſentatives and direct taxes ſhall be apportioned among the ſeveral ſtates which may be included within this Union, according to their reſpective numbers, which ſhall be determined by adding to the whole number of free perſons, including thoſe bound to ſervice for a term of years, and excluding Indians not taxed, three-fifths of all other perſons. The actual enumeration ſhall be made within three years after the firſt meeting of the Congreſs of the United States, and within every ſubſequent term of ten years, in ſuch manner as they ſhall by law direct. The number of repreſentatives ſhall not exceed one for every thirty thouſand, but each ſtate ſhall have at leaſt one repreſentative; and until ſuch enumeration ſhall be made, the ſtate of New-Hampſhire ſhall be entitled to chuſe three, Maſſachuſetts eight, Rhode-Iſland and Providence Plantations one, Connecticut five, New-York ſix, New-Jerſey four, Pennſylvania eight, Delaware one, Maryland ſix, Virginia ten, North-Carolina five, South-Carolina five, and Georgia three.

When vacancies happen in the repreſentation from any ſtate, the Executive authority thereof ſhall iſſue writs of election to fill ſuch vacancies.

The Houſe of Repreſentatives ſhall chuſe their Speaker and other officers; and ſhall have the ſole power of impeachment.

Sect. 3. The Senate of the United States ſhall be compoſed of two ſenators from each ſtate, choſen by the legiſlature thereof, for ſix years; and each ſenator ſhall have one vote.

Immediately after they ſhall be aſſembled in conſequence of the firſt election, they ſhall be divided as equally as may be into three claſſes. The ſeats of the ſenators of the firſt claſs ſhall be vacated at the expiration of the ſecond year, of the ſecond claſs at the expiration of the fourth year, and of the third claſs at the expiration of the ſixth year, ſo that one-third may be choſen every ſecond year; and if vacancies happen by reſignation, or otherwiſe, during the receſs of the Legiſlature of any ſtate, the Executive thereof may make temporary appointments until the next meeting of the Legiſlature, which ſhall then fill ſuch vacancies.

No perſon ſhall be a ſenator who ſhall not have attained to the age of thirty years, and been nine years a citizen of the United States, and who ſhall not, when elected, be an inhabitant of that ſtate for which he ſhall be choſen.

The Vice-Preſident of the United States ſhall be Preſident of the ſenate, but ſhall have no vote, unleſs they be equally divided.

The Senate ſhall chuſe their other officers, and alſo a Preſident pro tempore, in the abſence of the Vice-Preſident, or when he ſhall exerciſe the office of Preſident of the United States.

The Senate ſhall have the ſole power to try all impeachments. When ſitting for that purpoſe, they ſhall be on oath or affirmation. When the Preſident of the United States is tried, the Chief Juſtice ſhall preſide: And no perſon ſhall be convicted without the concurrence of two-thirds of the members preſent.

Judgment in caſes of impeachment ſhall not extend further than to removal from office, and diſqualification to hold and enjoy any office of honor, truſt or profit under the United States; but the party convicted ſhall nevertheleſs be liable and ſubject to indictment, trial, judgment and puniſhment, according to law.

Sect. 4. The times, places and manner of holding elections for ſenators and repreſentatives, ſhall be preſcribed in each ſtate by the legiſlature thereof; but the Congreſs may at any time by law make or alter ſuch regulations, except as to the places of chuſing Senators.

The Congreſs ſhall aſſemble at leaſt once in every year, and ſuch meeting ſhall be on the firſt Monday in December, unleſs they ſhall by law appoint a different day.

Sect. 5. Each houſe ſhall be the judge of the elections, returns and qualifications of its own members, and a majority of each ſhall conſtitute a quorum to do buſineſs; but a ſmaller number may adjourn from day to day, and may be authoriſed to compel the attendance of abſent members, in ſuch manner, and under ſuch penalties as each houſe may provide.

Each houſe may determine the rules of its proceedings, puniſh its members for diſorderly behaviour, and, with the concurrence of two-thirds, expel a member.

Each houſe ſhall keep a journal of its proceedings, and from time to time publiſh the ſame, excepting ſuch parts as may in their judgment require ſecrecy; and the yeas and nays of the members of either houſe on any queſtion ſhall, at the deſire of one-fifth of thoſe preſent, be entered on the journal.

Neither houſe, during the ſeſſion of Congreſs, ſhall, without the conſent of the other, adjourn for more than three days, nor to any other place than that in which the two houſes ſhall be ſitting.

Sect. 6. The ſenators and repreſentatives ſhall receive a compenſation for their ſervices, to be aſcertained by law, and paid out of the treaſury of the United States. They ſhall in all caſes, except treaſon, felony and breach of the peace, be privileged from arreſt during their attendance at the

so people greeted the publication of the Constitution with intense interest. Many were horrified by what they read. These Americans saw a repudiation of the ideals of 1776. The proposed government seemed too strong, too removed from local concerns, and too likely to be dominated by the rich and powerful. The federal government would "consolidate" the states out of existence. The presidency resembled a "foetus of monarchy." Unlike most state constitutions, the federal Constitution contained no bill of rights protecting civil liberties.

The Antifederalists also found a potent objection in republican theory. Republicanism had first appeared in the city-states of the ancient world. Republican government, the philosophers maintained, could flourish only within a small and homogeneous sphere. Only a tyrannical government could exercise authority over a nation as large and diverse as the United States. Such doubts had been expressed on the floor of the convention itself.

But nationalist momentum proved irresistible. Four states, including Pennsylvania, ratified before 1787 ended. The Federalists had energy and organization, and the best writers and politicians. They had Great Washington's support, and Ben Franklin's too. The Federalists also had few scruples about resorting to all manner of unsavory gambits in the state conventions. Connecticut ratified just after New Year's 1788. Massachusetts, one of the crucial big states, ratified in February 1788. Maryland ratified in April, South Carolina in May. New Hampshire ratified on June 21—the ninth state, thereby making the Constitution effective. Virginia ratified four days later, after rancorous debate. New York came in on a close vote in July.

And so the world learned that a new nation had appeared on history's stage. How long that nation might endure, none could say.

We the People of the United States..., **Philadelphia, 1787.**
(The Gilder Lehrman Collection, on deposit at the Pierpont Morgan Library: GLC 3585)
Delegate Benjamin Franklin inscribed this copy of the first official printing of the U.S. Constitution, known as the "Members' Edition." On September 17, 1787, the completed document was signed and sent to the states for ratification.

President

◆●●◆

$\mathcal{S}$OME MERIT may be accorded the proposition that George Washington had become a virtual head of state in 1775, that taking the oath as first president in 1789 was but a constitutional confirmation of his preeminence. For almost fifteen years Washington had been the most influential man in America. He had repeatedly displayed political skills of the highest order. As commander of the Continental Army, he had performed brilliantly as a statesman and diplomat, his talents here surpassing his military achievements. The Continental Congress had been only a provisional government, and an ineffective one at that. General Washington had been guided by no national executive, no minister of war, no secretary of state. Those duties had often devolved on him. In 1775, the colonists were deeply suspicious of standing armies, and the states remained intensely jealous of one another. The Continental Army was to remain in the field throughout the war. To command such an army, made up of thousands of men from the various colonies, had required an extraordinary leader. Though the tribulations of the presidency

George Washington, autograph letter to Richard Conway, March 4, 1789.

(Pierpont Morgan Library: MA 878)

Washington had to borrow money to settle debts and cover the costs of his trip to his inauguration. "Never 'till within these last two y[ea]rs I have experienced the want of money," Washington explained to a neighbor named Richard Conway. "Under this statement I am inclined to do what I have never expected to be reduced to the necessity of doing— that is, to borrow money upon interest." Conway lent the president-elect £600.

mounted quickly, the office that Washington accepted in 1789 probably presented a less daunting challenge than the one he had taken in 1775.

The Constitution provided that an electoral college select the president. The electors, chosen by the states, each would possess two votes, and each vote would be given a different candidate. The man getting the most votes would be president, and the runner-up would be vice president. The first electoral college was chosen in January 1789 and made its decision the following month. George Washington was elected by unanimous vote. That is, every elector cast one of his two votes for Washington. John Adams of Massachusetts was elected vice president, becoming first occupant of what Adams called the "most insignificant office that ever the invention of man contrived."

The capital was New York City, seat of the expiring Confederation Congress. Washington had to borrow £600 to pay his way to his inauguration. He left Mount Vernon on April 16, 1789. Two weeks earlier, the president-elect had written to a friend that "my movements to the chair of Government will be accompanied by feelings not unlike those of a culprit who is going to the place of his execution; so unwilling am I, in the evening of a life nearly consumed in public cares, to quit a peaceful Abode for an Ocean of difficulties, without that competency of political skill—abilities & inclination which is necessary to manage the helm." His reservations were quite sincere, as they had been at similar junctures in the past, but Washington had long since accepted the inevitability of the new assignment. His prestige was again indispensable. George Washington's hopes for the new nation, and the preservation of his own fame, left him no more choice than he had seen in 1775.

Pageantry attended his progress to New York. Nearly the entire population of Philadelphia turned out to welcome him. Balls, banquets, mass meetings, and parades were held in his honor. Soldiers marched, guns fired, choirs sang, poets declaimed, and churchmen prayed. An elaborate device contrived to drop a victor's laurel crown on Washington's head as white-robed maidens threw rose petals beneath his horse's hooves. The triumphal procession alarmed Washington as much as it gratified him. All his life he had pursued fame and hungered for acclaim. But sensible people can be discomfited by effusive praise, and the wise understand that fame is treacherous. This renewed adulation frightened him, for it seemed to carry with it the expectation of ever greater successes. Despite all he had achieved, Washington could never escape his morbid fear of failure.

The diary he kept at the time contains some of the most self-revealing passages that ever came from his pen: "I bade adieu to Mount Vernon, to private life, and to domestic felicity; and with a mind oppressed by more anxious and painful sensations than I have words to express, set out to New York...with the best dispositions to render service to my country in obedience to its

Mount Vernon April 1st. 1789

My dear Sir,

The Mail of the 30th. brought me your
favor of the 23d. — For which, & the regular information
you have had the goodness to transmit of the state of
things in New York, I feel myself very much obliged,
and thank you accordingly. —

I feel for those Members of the new Congress,
who, hitherto, have given an unavailing attendance
at the theatre of business. — For myself, the delay may
be compared to a reprieve; for in confidence I can
assure you — with the world it would obtain little
credit — that my movements to the chair of Government will be accompanied with feelings not unlike those of a culprit who is going to the place
of his execution: so unwilling am I, in the evening of a life nearly consumed in public cares,
to quit a peaceful abode for an Ocean of difficulties, without that competency of political
skill — abilities & inclination which is necessary to manage
the helm. — I am sensible, that I am embarking
the voice of my Countrymen and a good name
of my own, on this voyage, but what returns
will be made for them — Heaven alone can
foretell. — Integrity & firmness is all I can promise — these, be the voyage long or short, never
shall forsake me although I may be deserted
by all men. — For of the consolations, which are
to be derived from these (under any circumstances) the world cannot deprive me. —
With best wishes for Mrs. Knox, & sincere friendship for yourself — I remain

Your affectionate
G: Washington

The Honble
Majr. Genl. Knox

call, but with less hope of answering its expectations." After crossing the Hudson, he wrote, "The display of boats which attended and joined us on this occasion, some with vocal and some with instrumental music on board; the roar of cannon, and the loud acclamations of the people which rent the skies, as I passed along the wharves, filled my mind with sensations as painful (considering the reverse of the scene, which may be the case after all my labors to do good) as they are pleasing." Washington's fears were prophetic. The presidency would cost him enormous anguish.

He took the oath of office on the balcony of Federal Hall, overlooking Wall Street, on April 30, 1789. An official cried, "Long live George Washington, President of the United States!" The crowd cheered. One witness remembered that Washington's hand trembled and his voice shook as he read his inaugural address. Here he repeated what he had often said before, that the

George Washington, autograph letter to Henry Knox, April 1, 1789.
(The Gilder Lehrman Collection, on deposit at the Pierpont Morgan Library: GLC 2437 LIII, 69)
In this remarkable letter to a friend, Washington poured out his fears as he prepared to risk his hard-won fame by taking on the presidency: "In confidence I can assure *you*… that my movements to the chair of Government will be accompanied by feelings not unlike those of a culprit who is going to the place of his execution: so unwilling am I, in the evening of a life nearly consumed in public cares, to quit a peaceful Abode for an Ocean of difficulties, without that competency of political skill—abilities & inclination which is necessary to manage the helm. I am sensible, that I am embarking the voice of my Countrymen and a good name of my own, on this voyage, but what returns will be made for them—Heaven alone can foretell."

Commemorative clothing buttons worn by spectators at Washington's inauguration, 1789.
(National Museum of American History, Smithsonian Institution: 227739.1789. 1 and 1980.0771.02)
The more elaborate example is engraved with the seal of the United States and the legend "March the Fourth 1789. Memorable Era." Although the Constitution set March 4 as inauguration day, the first president could not be sworn in until April 30.

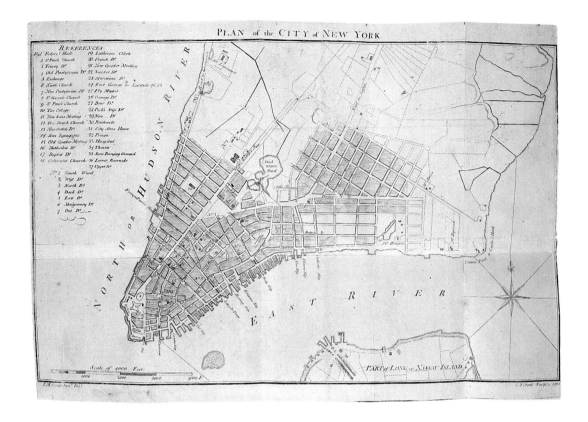

"destiny of the Republican model of Government [is] staked, on the experiment entrusted to the hands of the American people."

With only Congress and the president himself in office, there was at first little work for the chief executive. Still, Washington was concerned about his every action. "I walk on untrodden ground," he said. "There is scarcely any part of my conduct wch may not hereafter be drawn into precedent." Kings people understood; presidents were another matter altogether. In all the western world, no elected head of state exercised substantial powers. Washington must now bridge the decisive shift from kingship to an executive authority derived from the people.

Fortunately for the new president, Congress settled the awkward matter of an official title, spurning a monarchical "His Highness the President of the United States of America and Protector of Their Liberties" for the republican simplicity of "Mr. President." But George Washington, who hated monarchy, would never escape

"Plan of the City of New York," in *New-York Directory . . . for 1789.* **New York, 1789.**
(Huntington Library: 15038)
New York was the first capital of the United States. The city's thirty-three thousand inhabitants crowded onto the southern tip of Manhattan Island.

"View of the Federal Edifice in New York," in *The Massachusetts Magazine, . . .May, 1789,* **Boston, 1789.**

(Huntington Library: 251823)

On April 30, 1789, George Washington took the oath as first president of the United States on the balcony of Federal Hall overlooking Wall Street. Subscribers to *The Massachusetts Magazine* could read about the ceremony and study this elevation of the building on a folding plate.

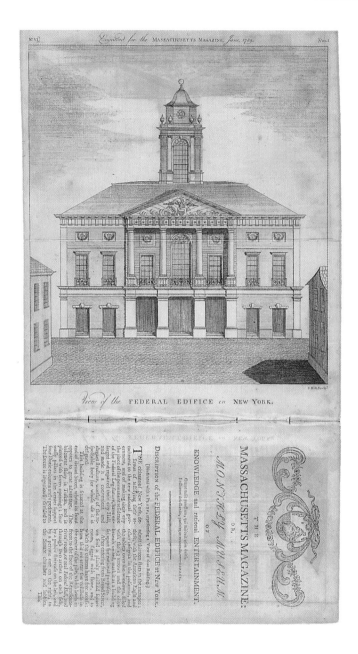

accusations of harboring monarchical ambitions. From the beginning of his presidency, and ever more often as the numbers of his detractors grew, Washington would be charged with taking on regal airs, even lusting to be the first American king.

The cold face that Washington habitually turned to the world was both an expression of his self-doubt and a constructed public persona that had enabled him to exercise power for decades.

His enemies, however, would equate aloofness with regal pretensions. The lavish life that the president and his family enjoyed in their rented New York mansion was no more opulent than what they had been accustomed to at Mount Vernon, but ostentation provided fuel for critics. The weekly receptions that Washington staged to guard his working hours from a stream of unannounced callers were painfully stiff affairs, offensive to the republican sensibilities of many. George Washington was extraordinarily sensitive to criticism, and for some time his stature had largely protected him. But he soon realized that the presidency would draw attacks as surely as Dr. Franklin's lightning rod pulled bolts from the sky.

The Philadelphia Convention had outlined a skeletal government. It was up to Congress to put flesh on the bare bones. The Constitution contained only a single reference to the "principal Officer in each of the executive Departments." It did not say who would appoint those officers or control those departments. But Congress voted to put the departments of state, war, and the treasury under the president. Secretaries of the departments were to be nominated by the president and confirmed by the Senate. After some debate, it was agreed that the president need not require the Senate's consent to remove his secretaries, another significant gain for executive authority.

Washington appointed Alexander Hamilton secretary of the treasury, Henry Knox secretary of war, and Thomas Jefferson secretary of state. The Senate confirmed them. Within this first presidential cabinet were the seeds of the discord that would rend the Washington administration and the nation itself.

There was more untrodden ground to cross. The Constitution gave the president power "by and with the Advice and Consent of the Senate, to make Treaties, provided two-thirds of the Senators present concur." But what form should this advice and consent take? Should the president work out the terms of pending treaties with the Senate? The Constitution did not say. The test case proved to be a treaty with the southern Creek tribe in

August 1789. Washington had asked James Madison how to proceed—"would an Oral or written communication be best? If the first what mode is to be adopted to effect it?" Washington and a committee of senators soon decided that "In all matters respecting Treaties, oral communications seem indispensably necessary." The Senate wanted an active role in the formulation of treaties and foreign policy. President Washington concurred.

But the collaboration did not go smoothly when the president

George Washington, autograph letter to James Madison, August 5, 1789.

(Huntington Library: HM 5100)

President Washington consulted Madison, the Father of the Constitution, on the workings of that untried document. The Constitution required the president to make foreign treaties with the "Advice and Consent of the Senate." But no one could say what form "Advice and Consent" should take. The president asked Madison "would an Oral or written communication be best?" Washington's single attempt to negotiate a treaty with the Senate failed and has never been repeated by any of his presidential successors.

visited the Senate chamber on August 22. After the lengthy document had been read aloud, the senators requested a postponement until they could consider the papers before them. Washington became angry. One senator recalled that "the President of the U.S. started up in a Violent fret. 'This defeats every purpose of my coming here,' were the first words he said." Washington agreed to return two days later. But for the last time—the arrangement was unworkable. Leaving the second session, the president was heard to mutter that he'd "be damned if he ever went there again!" In the two hundred and ten years since, neither George Washington nor any of his presidential successors has returned to negotiate with the Senate. The Senate's role has been confined to ratification of treaties formulated by the president. The episode set a precedent that helped establish foreign policy as the president's domain. But Washington had demonstrated again that he respected the Constitution and the powers of Congress.

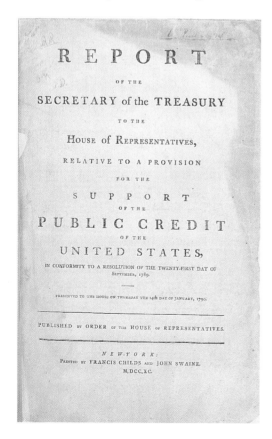

Alexander Hamilton, *Report . . . to the House of Representatives . . . for the Support of the public credit of the United States,* **New York, 1790.**

(The Gilder Lehrman Collection, on deposit at the Pierpont Morgan Library: GLC 960)

Treasury Secretary Hamilton's fiscal program helped make the United States a great nation. But many Republicans feared that Hamilton plotted to create a corrupt aristocratic regime that would subvert liberty.

George Washington was convinced that political parties ("factions") were a source of corrupting evil, perhaps the gravest threat the new nation faced. The first president believed that government leaders must be elected on their reputations for disinterested public service. A republican statesman's only aim should be the good of the nation as a whole. He must pursue no partisan program. It is ironic, then, that the 1790s emerged as the Age of Passion—the most fervently partisan decade in American history. At the heart of the conflict was the clash of two fundamentally opposed conceptions of the American experiment.

The human poles around which the two proto-parties began to coalesce were Secretary of the Treasury Alexander Hamilton and Secretary of State Thomas Jefferson. Both were men of rare genius. They were the two ranking officials in the president's administration. Rivalry quickly moved beyond ideology to burning personal animosity—the most memorable of all American political feuds. Warfare in the bosom of his official family drove Washington to despair.

The Hamiltonian party came to be called Federalist, the Jeffersonian Republican (or Democratic-Republican). It was no accident that the Hamiltonians took up the name used by supporters of the Constitution. The Federalists saw themselves as extending the nationalist movement to build a strong government. They looked toward a consolidated nation in which federal authority would stand above that of the states. The Hamiltonians supported banking and investment, trade and commerce, and solid national credit. The big cities of the North were their natural realm. They intended that the United States become a great nation, a power among the powers of earth. Federalists openly admired Great Britain for the stability of its government and the soundness of its financial system. Did they also favor the British monarchical model of government for the United States?

Jefferson and his Republican followers certainly thought so. They found their spiritual home among the fields of rural America,

BANK OF THE UNITED STATES, in Third Street PHILADELPHIA.

especially the plantations of the slaveholding South. Jefferson named those who turned the soil the "chosen people of God." His vision of the American future took in an agrarian utopia in which generation after generation of sturdy farmers passed honest, independent lives, far from cities and scheming money men. Jefferson favored states' rights over federal authority. Government should be limited and local. Tyranny was to be feared more than anarchy. His faith in the common people was unbounded. The well-born author of the Declaration of Independence loved republican equality as much as the self-made treasury secretary admired aristocracy. Jeffersonians hated banks and financial speculations as the fountain of corruption in public and private affairs. They were passionate supporters of the republican revolution that had broken out in France. The Republicans believed that the Hamiltonians aimed at

William Birch, "Bank of the United States," in *The City of Philadelphia*, Philadelphia, 1800.

(Huntington Library: 305000, plate 17)

Hamilton's Bank of the United States, and the vision of America's future that it implied, were abhorrent to Virginia Republicans like Thomas Jefferson and James Madison. But their fellow Virginian President Washington endorsed Hamilton's plan and signed the bank bill into law.

nothing less than the creation of an American aristocracy. Some of Washington's conduct that seemed to smack of monarchical pretensions now appeared all the more alarming to fearful Republicans. They pondered the president's magisterial aloofness, the very grandeur of his person, the stateliness of the presidential household, with its thirty servants, and the awesome formality of his weekly "levees." People wondered if this was evidence that Washington secretly supported Hamilton's aristocratic schemes, or at the least, that the president was Hamilton's unwitting tool.

Alexander Hamilton had done little to ease such fears. Many remembered his day-long speech extolling constitutional monarchy at the Philadelphia Convention in 1787. He had not hesitated to declare the British constitution the "most perfect in the world." Jefferson believed that the Hamiltonians regarded the new government as a mere "stepping stone" to a state in which the influence of the powerful would again overshadow human equality. If republican government faltered, as many expected, Hamilton was sure to gain converts. But both Hamilton and Jefferson understood that George Washington was

Order of Procession, to be Observed on the Arrival of the President.... Providence, August 17, 1790, **Providence, 1790.**

(Huntington Library: 108388)

Americans who feared a betrayal of their Revolution's republican principles were alarmed by elaborate presidential ceremonies that seemed to recall the monarchical pomp of Europe.

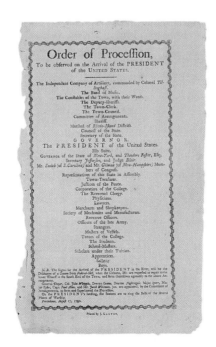

unswerving in his dedication to republicanism and to an indissoluble union of the states.

The great schism opened in 1790, when the secretary of the treasury submitted his plan to establish a financial system for the United States. Federal government would take on all the public debts incurred in the Revolutionary War. The national war debt was about $54 million. Hamilton also proposed that the government assume the state war debts—an additional $25 million. The funding bill would create a permanent national debt on which the United States would pay interest. The resulting treasury notes would offer investments for those with ready cash. Interest payments would be funded by taxes and duties. Hamilton presently called for the creation of the Bank of the United States, which would issue paper money backed by gold, vastly increasing the circulating currency available for business and commerce.

Much of the Hamiltonian program—perpetual federal debt and taxation, banks, investments, and paper money—was anathema to the Republicans. Financial speculation would debauch politics, the North would benefit instead of the South, and commerce and industry would be exalted at the expense of the agrarian class. Galling to Virginians like Congressman Madison was that their state, which had already paid down its war debt, would not benefit from federal assumption as would the northern states, which had large outstanding debts. The Republicans blocked the funding bill in Congress. But the opponents soon made a deal.

The site of the capital of the United States had not been fixed. Southerners (not least among them President Washington) looked for a national capital on the Potomac. North of that river, most people thought that choosing New York or Philadelphia more sensible than building a whole new city. The Virginians agreed to pass the funding bill in exchange for locating the "Federal City" on the Potomac. The capital would move from New York to Philadelphia for ten years while the new city was building. Government would transfer to its permanent seat in 1800.

[Andrew Ellicot], *Plan of the city of Washington . . . Seat of Government after the Year [1800]*, Philadelphia, 1792.

(Huntington Library: 443542)
George Washington raised no objection to the decision to name the new federal capital "Washington, the District of Columbia." He personally picked a site about ten miles from Mount Vernon and made sure that a grand metropolis, worthy of a great nation, was laid out. But generations would pass before the muddy village on the Potomac became a great city.

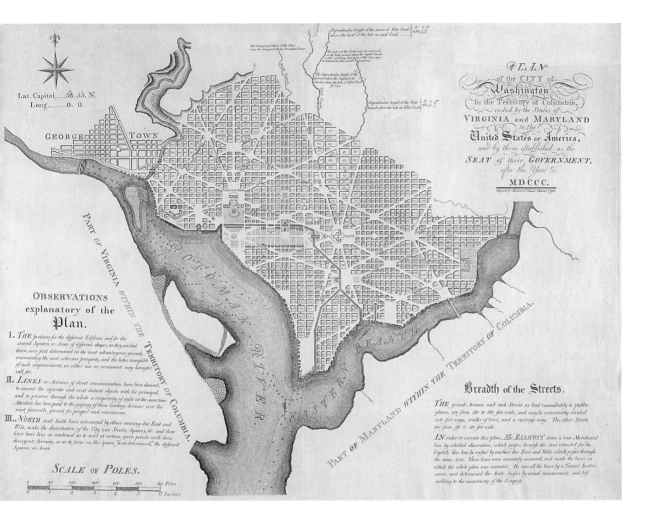

President Washington threw himself into the project. He picked a site only a few miles from Mount Vernon. Nothing suggests that Washington objected to the decision to name the capital after him. The victory seemed to crown his lifelong pursuit of economic development and national preeminence for his home district and the great river on whose banks he had first drawn breath. He believed that the Potomac canal would bring the harvests of the Ohio Valley over the mountains. He was certain that Washington, the District of Columbia, was destined to become the greatest city in America.

"The Spirit of Party" now ruled in the temporary capital at Philadelphia. Partisan newspapers appeared. (Jefferson kept his

house editor on the state department payroll as a translator.) Leading characters like Hamilton and Madison exchanged fire by pseudonymous essay in the columns of the *Gazette of the United States* and the *National Gazette*. Republicans found it increasingly difficult to attack Hamilton and the Federalist fiscal program without spilling their censures onto Washington himself.

The president appeared to be taking the Federalist line. When Jefferson and Madison urged him to veto the bank bill as unconstitutional, Washington decided in favor of Hamilton's interpretation of the Constitution's "implied powers" and signed the Bank of the United States into being. Washington had grown disillusioned with slavery and the agrarianism that Jefferson so admired. War and government had given him broad experience in the northern states, and he recognized the northern cities as the vital centers of commerce and government in the modern world. He favored energetic government, standing armies, and strong national credit. Washington was not pleased that his fellow

[Attributed to Nicholas King, view of the President's House, Treasury Department, and Blodgett's Hotel, Washington, D.C., c. 1810.]

(Huntington Library: HM 52665) Probably executed within a decade of George Washington's death, this sketch suggests the rustic character of the little national capital named in his honor. The President's House and the Treasury Department appear between the trees in the distance. Blodgett's Hotel, the brick building at the right, proved large enough to house most of the federal government after the British burned Washington in 1814.

CONGRESS HALL and NEW THEATRE, in Chesnut Street PHILADELPHIA.

Drawn, Engraved & Published by W. Birch & Son, Neshaminy Bridge, 1800.

William Birch, "Congress Hall," in *The City of Philadelphia,* **Philadelphia, 1800.**

(Huntington Library: 305000, plate 20)

The government moved from New York to Philadelphia in 1790, and it was there that Washington served out most of his presidency. George Washington is the only chief executive never to have presided in the capital that bears his name.

Virginians consistently opposed the measures he deemed vital to national success. He was angered by suggestions in the opposition press that he did not really approve Hamilton's plans, for that implied, the president complained, that he was "too careless to attend them or too stupid to understand them." His efforts to reconcile Jefferson and Hamilton failed.

Washington wanted out. He had taken the office cheered by the hope that he might be permitted to return to Mount Vernon after just a year or two, as soon as the new government was running smoothly. No such prospect appeared on the political horizon, but he still intended to resign when his term ended in 1793. In May 1792 he asked Madison to help him prepare a farewell address. Those who suspect that George Washington's great state papers were the work of other minds would do well to examine this letter.

George Washington, autograph letter to James Madison, May 20, 1792.

(Pierpont Morgan Library: MA 505)

President Washington wanted to leave office when his first term ended in 1793. He asked Madison to help him write a farewell address to announce his decision to retire. But Madison and other statesmen soon convinced Washington that he was obliged to continue as president. The new country and the fragile union could not survive the embittered partisan battle for the presidency that Washington's departure was sure to bring.

President Washington told Madison what he wanted to say. He was enlisting the services of an editor, not a ghostwriter.

Madison reluctantly drafted the address but told Washington that his resignation would be a national catastrophe. Others gave the same advice. By 1792, Alexander Hamilton and Thomas Jefferson concurred in little but their antipathy for one another, but they did agree that the fragile union could never survive the bitterly contested presidential election that Washington's retirement was sure to bring. "North & South will hang together, if they have you to hang on," Jefferson promised. The president had assured Madison that he would not step down if it seemed that his "deriliction of the Chair of Government [would] involve the Country in serious disputes...& disagreeable consequences."

George Washington, autograph letter to Henry Lee, January 20, 1793.

(The Gilder Lehrman Collection, on deposit at the Pierpont Morgan Library: GLC 2793.002)

George Washington quipped that he regretted taking a second presidential term only "once." Unfortunately, that "once," Washington continued, "was every moment since!" In this letter, Washington confided to a friend that he had decided to stay on only "after a long and painful conflict in my own breast."

The unhappy Washington was finally convinced ("after a long and painful conflict in my own breast") that he must stay on to save the great experiment. He was reelected unanimously.

Just before his second inauguration, the president spoke to Jefferson of the "extreme wretchedness of [my] existence while in office." A few months later, Washington told his secretary of state that he regretted "but once" having agreed to serve a second term. Unfortunately, that "once," Washington continued, was "every moment since." He swore that "*by God* he had rather be in his grave than in his present situation; he had rather be on his farm than be made *Emperor of the world;* and yet they were charging him with wanting to be a King."

The war that broke out between revolutionary France and monarchical Britain in 1793 raised political hatred in Philadelphia to extraordinary levels. President Washington issued his Proclamation of Neutrality in April 1793. But the Federalist and Republican

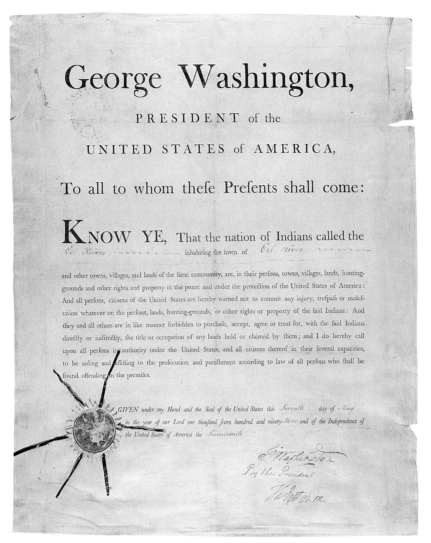

George Washington,
PRESIDENT of the
UNITED STATES of AMERICA,

To all to whom thefe Prefents shall come:

KNOW YE, That the nation of Indians called the
Eel Rivers inhabiting the town of *Eel river*

and other towns, villages, and lands of the fame community, are, in their perfons, towns, villages, lands, hunting-grounds and other rights and property in the peace and under the protection of the United States of America: And all perfons, citizens of the United States are hereby warned not to commit any injury, trefpafs or molef-tation whatever on the perfons, lands, hunting-grounds, or other rights or property of the faid Indians: And they and all others are in like manner forbidden to purchafe, accept, agree or treat for, with the faid Indians directly or indirectly, the title or occupation of any lands held or claimed by them; and I do hereby call upon all perfons in authority under the United States, and all citizens thereof in their feveral capacities, to be aiding and affifting to the profecution and punifhment according to law of all perfons who fhall be found offending in the premifes.

GIVEN under my Hand and the Seal of the United States this *Seventh* day of *May* in the year of our Lord one thoufand feven hundred and ninety-*three* and of the Independence of the United States of America the *Seventeenth*

George Washington
By the President
Th: Jefferson

George Washington, document signed, May 7, 1793.

(Huntington Library: HM 5550) President Washington gave a delegation of Miami Indians this proclamation promising that the United States would protect the tribe's land. But despite the promises, soon there would be no Miami people living on the banks of the Wabash River. Like the other native peoples of the Ohio Valley, the Miamis would be dispossessed.

factions were anything but impartial. The Hamiltonians of course supported England, the Jeffersonians France.

Since Washington did not take the side of America's sister republic, the friends of France charged that he must be a sup-porter of Britain, and hence Hamilton's ally in the ghastly con-spiracy to establish an aristocratic regime in the United States. Republican propagandists now had no scruples about attacking the president. Certain thoughtful editors even remembered to send Washington free copies of their denunciations. These attacks both enraged and deeply wounded the president, particu-

Drawn Engraved & Published by W. Birch. & Son   Sold by R. Campbell &C°. N° 30 Chesnut Street Philad? 1799.

BACK of the STATE HOUSE, PHILADELPHIA.

William Birch, "Back of the State House," in *The City of Philadelphia*, Philadelphia, 1800.

(Huntington Library: 305000, plate 22)

A party of native Americans, perhaps an official delegation on a visit to the president, explores the grounds of Independence Hall, meeting place of Congress during the 1790s.

larly when he considered how unwillingly he had consented to stay in office. Jefferson believed that Washington was hurt by criticism more than any other public figure. His obsession with his reputation had never waned.

Washington had embraced neutrality to preserve the United States, but many Republicans and Federalists were too caught up in their ideologies to understand. Washington's grasp of the realities of power in international affairs greatly exceeded that of most of his contemporaries. Neutrality was not a tactic that the Federalists might use to align America with Britain, or a weapon for the Republicans to employ on behalf of France. Neutrality was a means of buying time for America. The United States was simply too weak and unstable to become embroiled in European wars.

Taking sides in the present conflict would be all the more disastrous in light of the political struggle at home.

Washington believed that the United States would attain a stature of unassailable strength if allowed to develop peacefully. But he dreaded war in the 1790s. He reminded his ambassador to France that "unwise we should be in the extreme to involve ourselves in the contests of European Nations, where our weight could be but small; tho; the loss to ourselves certain." Washington's hope for his people was that "instead of being Frenchmen, or Englishmen, in Politics, they would be Americans; indignant at every attempt of either, or any other power to establish an influence in our Councils."

But ideology continued to divide Americans. Pro-French Democratic-Republican Societies sprang up. George Washington was convinced that the societies were subversive. In the summer of 1794 disgruntled farmers in western Pennsylvania violently resisted the collection of the hated federal excise tax on distilled spirits. The president mistakenly believed that the Whiskey Rebellion had been fomented by outsiders. "I consider this insurrection the first *formidable* fruit of the Democratic Societies," he wrote. The uprisings collapsed without further bloodshed when he led twelve thousand militia into the region. It was an army larger than he had commanded during most of the Revolution. The president dismayed Republicans like James Madison when he repeated his charges against the "self-created societies" in his Annual Message at year's end. Jefferson resigned, depriving the president of a valuable counterweight to Hamilton in the cabinet.

Political dissension intensified in 1795. Despite the neutrality proclamation, both France and Britain attacked American shipping. When war with England threatened, Washington dispatched a special envoy, John Jay, to London. The result of those negotiations, Jay's Treaty, reached the president in March 1795. Washington was not pleased with the terms. Mighty Britain had conceded little to its former colonies. But adopting the "Treaty of

George Washington, manuscript signed (draft of the 1794 Annual Message), November 1794.
(The Gilder Lehrman Collection, on deposit at the Pierpont Morgan Library: GLC 1054)
This is the president's own copy of his 1794 Annual Message, the report now known as the State of the Union Address. Washington asserted that the state of the union in 1794 was precarious. He was alarmed by the recent Whiskey Rebellion in western Pennsylvania. The president mistakenly believed that the uprising had been fomented by opponents of his administration from the new "Democratic-Republican Societies."

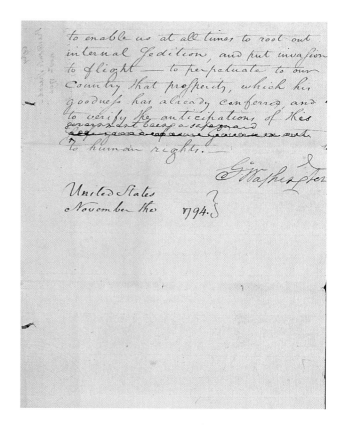

Fellow Citizens of the Senate, and of the House of Representatives.

When we call to mind the gracious indulgence of Heaven, by which the American people became a nation, when we survey the general prosperity of our Country, and look forward to the riches, power and happiness to which it seems destined; with the deepest regret do I announce to you, that during your recess some of the Citizens of the United States, have been found capable of an insurrection. It is due, however, to the character of our government and to its stability, which cannot be shaken by the enemies of order freely to unfold the course of this event.

During the Session of 1790

to enable us at all times to root out internal Sedition, and put invasion to flight — to perpetuate to our Country that prosperity, which his goodness has already conferred, and to verify the anticipations of this government being a safeguard to human rights. —

G.º Washington

United States November the 1794.

Amity, Commerce and Navigation, between his Britannic Majesty, and the United States of America" would avert war and give American vessels a little more freedom to trade. And London had agreed to one important American demand—Britain would finally give up its military presence in the Northwest Territory.

Washington was not sure whether he should push for the treaty's ratification. Even the Federalists recognized that the British diplomats had handled Jay roughly. The Republicans of course vehemently opposed any agreement with England. Did not a peace treaty with one belligerent amount to a declaration of war against the other? The president sent the treaty to the Senate, where it was debated and ratified in secret session. But soon the text was leaked and published by the opposition. Furious denunciations, riots, even attacks on federal officials followed. Republicans charged that the administration was treacherously surrendering to England. But

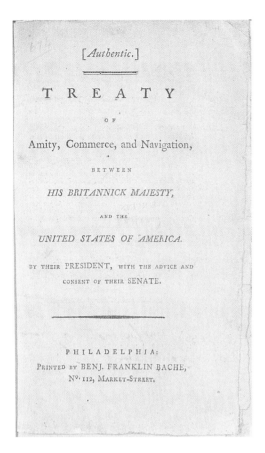

Treaty of Amity, Commerce, and Navigation, between His Britannick Majesty, and the United States of America..., **Philadelphia, 1795.**
(Huntington Library: 66613)
The secret text of Jay's Treaty with Britain was leaked to the opposition press and published in this "authentic" pamphlet.

Washington signed the treaty and won a hard-fought battle in the House for the funding to put it into action. In this fight he was aided by the victory that the United States had achieved in the treaty with Spain. That treaty permitted American settlers in the west to use the Mississippi to trade through New Orleans. When the House of Representatives demanded that he turn over secret diplomatic papers relating to the treaty with Britain, the president invoked executive privilege for the first time and refused to surrender the papers. In his written response, Washington acidly observed that he had, after all, been present at the drafting of Constitution and knew as well as anyone that the document gave the lower house no role in the formulation of foreign policy.

By the end of his presidency all semblance of harmony had vanished. The opposition press called Washington a "supercilious tyrant." "If ever a Nation was debauched by a man," the same

Thomas Paine, *Letter to George Washington...,* Philadelphia, 1796.

(Huntington Library: 7802)

By the end of Washington's second term, the president's foes were leveling the most scathing attacks against him. Thomas Paine, who had once lionized General Washington, now denounced President Washington as a lying tyrant. "As to you, sir," Paine wrote in this pamphlet, "the world will be puzzled to decide, whether you have abandoned good principles, or whether you ever had any."

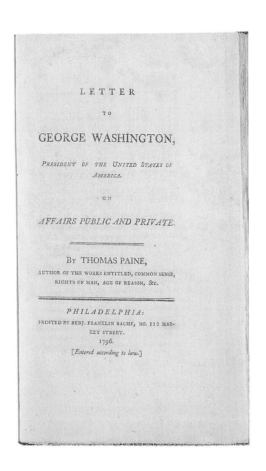

paper informed its readers, "the American Nation has been debauched by Washington." One of the harshest blasts came from the Revolution's most celebrated pamphleteer. In the dark days of 1776, Thomas Paine had extolled General Washington as liberty's God-given savior. Twenty years later, the radical revolutionary savaged the president in his widely circulated *Letter to George Washington.* "Elevated to the chair of the Presidency, you assumed the merit of everything to yourself," Paine hissed. "You commenced your Presidential career by encouraging, and swallowing, the grossest adulation.... As to you, sir, treacherous in private friendship... and a hypocrite in public life, the world will be puzzled to decide, whether you have abandoned good principles, or whether you ever had any."

British withdrawal from the Northwest Territory furthered American ambitions in the Ohio Valley. Britain had kept garrisons

MAD TOM in A RAGE

Mad Tom in a Rage.

(Huntington Library: cartoon collection)

This Federalist cartoon depicts "Mad Tom" Paine as the malevolent despoiler of the federal edifice erected by Washington. Americans of the 1790s had not yet recognized the value of a loyal opposition. Like many of the ruling Federalists, President Washington sometimes believed that Republicans who opposed his policies were enemies of the union.

in the posts that English diplomats had promised to surrender in the peace treaty of 1783. From there, Englishmen had supplied the Indians with weapons and encouraged them to war against the Americans. Coalitions of the Ohio Valley tribes had convincingly defeated two U.S. armies. But General Anthony Wayne's 1794 victory at Fallen Timbers and the British exit now doomed the warriors' hopes of turning back the invasion. George Washington had promoted the settlement of the Ohio Valley for fifty years. He held no illusions about the fate of the native populations: they were to be dispossessed. Washington hoped that the takeover could be accomplished as peacefully as possible, but he wanted nothing to stop the flood of settlers pouring over the mountains.

In the spring of 1793, a delegation from the Miami tribe

Gilbert Stuart, *George Washington,* **1797.**

(The Virginia Steele Scott Collection, Huntington Art Collections: 39.1. Gift of Mrs. Alexander Baring, 1939)

Washington's face became a ubiquitous republican icon. It is unfortunate that Gilbert Stuart's "dollar bill" portrait of the grim, burned-out old man in his bitter second term has remained the universally recognized Washington. History is better served by the Jean-Antoine Houdon's 1785 sculpture of the vital younger man.

paid an official visit on President Washington in Philadelphia. These Indians lived far to the west, on the banks of the Wabash River. Washington gave the Miamis an imposing presidential proclamation, countersigned by Thomas Jefferson, and adorned with the beribboned seal of the United States. The creamy parchment promised that the government would protect the tribe's "persons, towns, villages, lands, hunting-grounds and other rights and properties." Washington handed out gleaming silver peace medals struck with the likeness of himself sharing a peace pipe with a chief. He promised friendship.

George Washington, ["The Farewell Address" with Washington's autograph notes], in *Claypoole's American Daily Advertiser*, Philadelphia, September 19, 1796.

(The Gilder Lehrman Collection, on deposit at the Pierpont Morgan Library: GLC 185)

Washington announced his decision to retire at the end of his second term by publishing the Farewell Address in a Philadelphia newspaper. Many had expected that the first president would stay in office until he died.

But there was one other point the president wished to communicate to the tribesmen. Washington also gave them a letter, addressed to "My Children," that contained this naked threat: "Most of you have been a long Journey to the Eastward where you have seen the numbers and Strength of a part of the United States. But you have seen only a part.... Judge then, what the bad Indians may expect in the end if they will not harken to the voice of peace!" The definition of "bad Indians" chosen by the United States proved to be exceedingly broad. The Miamis, like the other Ohio Valley tribes, would lose their homeland.

Early in 1796 the president dug out the farewell address that Madison had written four years before. This time Washington would not be deterred. He was going back to Mount Vernon when his second term ended in 1797. He was old and tired and disillusioned, and he was right in thinking that he did not have many more years to live. Using the passages that Madison had submitted, Washington drafted a lengthy address. Because Madison was his enemy now, the president sought out the editorial assistance of Alexander Hamilton, who had left the cabinet in

Sheraton-style side chair.

(National Museum of American History, Smithsonian Institution: 13152)

President Washington bought this chair from a Philadelphia cabinetmaker in 1797 and took it home to Mount Vernon.

Silver candlestick.

(National Museum of American History, Smithsonian Institution: 13152; 1182)

Candlestick purchased by George Washington in 1783 and used in the presidential households in New York and Philadelphia.

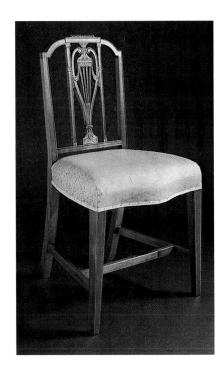

Oval silver tray.

(National Museum of American History, Smithsonian Institution: 13152; 1189)
Silver tray purchased by George Washington in 1783 and used in the presidential households in New York and Philadelphia.

Silver bottle stand.

(National Museum of American History, Smithsonian Institution: 13152; 1187)
Bottle stand purchased by George Washington in 1783 and used in the presidential households in New York and Philadelphia.

1795. Over the next few months the two men hammered out a text that satisfied Washington. He made public his decision to retire when the Farewell Address was printed in the *American Daily Advertiser,* a Philadelphia newspaper, on September 19, 1796.

Washington's Farewell Address soon achieved a monumentality that has encouraged some to regard it as a source of timeless wisdom. But its author had intended nothing of the sort. The document was a product of the political passions of the 1790s. Washington's audience comprised his countrymen, not the unborn Americans of future centuries. For George Washington did not know, and would die not knowing, whether the United States of America was destined to endure.

On first reading, the Farewell Address seems to deal with three dominant themes: the preservation of the union, foreign policy, and domestic politics. But foreign affairs and political factionalism at home constituted a single issue in Washington's mind—the only issue that threatened to wreck the union. The time was not far off, Washington predicted again, when the United States would be too strong for any European nation to threaten. But now the devotion of the American political factions to one or the other of the warring powers was so intense that the union could never survive if the United States allowed itself to become entangled in the struggle. Nations do not have natural friends or enemies, Washington insisted; nations only have interests. The American people must be Americans first. They must avoid "an habitual hatred, or an habitual fondness" for any foreign nation. Neutrality, the president concluded, had been his "endeavour to gain time for our country to settle and mature its yet recent institutions."

In spurning the entreaties of some Federalists that he stand for a third term, Washington established one more important precedent. Many had hoped or feared that he would stay in office until he died. As president for life, George Washington would have set a standard that many of his successors would surely have aspired to match. Instead, he handed over the presidency to John Adams on March 4, 1797. It must have been one of the happiest days of his life.

Chinese export porcelain covered cup from "a Box of China for Lady Washington."

(National Museum of American History, Smithsonian Institution)

This cup from the "States" china given to Martha Washington by an admirer in 1796 is ornamented with a chain of fifteen linked states, symbolizing the union, and her "MW" monogram.

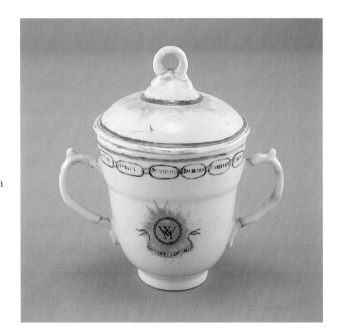

Farewell

———◆◆◆———

ASHINGTON'S RETURN to Mount Vernon in 1797 probably reminded him of his homecoming after the Revolution. Despite the hundreds of pages of instructions that he had sent his farm managers while president, he found affairs at home in disarray. He began the work of putting things right with exuberance: "I begin my diurnal course with the Sun," he wrote a friend. "If my hirelings are not in their places at that time I send them messages expressive of my sorrow for their indisposition; then having put these wheels in motion, I examine the state of things further; and the more they are probed, the deeper I find the wounds are which my buildings have sustained by an absence and neglect of eight years." Work at Mount Vernon and his endless letter-writing kept Washington busy from sunrise until he retired at nine o'clock.

The first former president of the United States watched uneasily as events in Europe continued to convulse America. By 1798 war with France appeared likely. Washington came to regard the Republicans who supported France and opposed the policies of

Pocket watch, English, 1793–94. Satin waistcoat.
(Mount Vernon Ladies' Association)
Washington acquired this gold watch while serving as president in Philadelphia. It rests on a quilted satin waistcoat worn by Washington.

President Adams as enemies of the union. Swayed by the passions of that extraordinary moment in American history, Washington had begun to confuse dissent with disloyalty. The figure who hated political parties scarcely recognized that he himself had become a hardline Federalist. At sixty-six, George Washington was an aged man. His memory, eyesight, and hearing were beginning to fail him. Some of his sober moderation and impeccable judgment had deserted him as well.

Congress authorized the raising of the New Army to meet the supposed threat of a French invasion. Without consulting Washington, President Adams commissioned the superannuated veteran a lieutenant general and gave him the command. Unfortunately, Washington believed that he owed his country this final duty. His command of the New Army stands out as the most melancholy episode in his career. Washington behaved badly: He quarreled with the president. He questioned the patriotism of the Republican

George Washington, autograph letter to Eliza Parke Custis, September 14, 1794.

(Pierpont Morgan Library: MA 503) Washington offered his step-granddaughter advice on love and marriage: "There are emotions of a softer kind, to wch. the heart of girl turned eighteen, is susceptible," he warned. "Do not… conceive, from the fine tales the Poets & lovers of old have told us, of the transports of mutual love, that heaven has taken its abode on earth: Nor do not deceive yourself in supposing that the only means by which these are to be obtained, is to drink deep of the cup, and revel in an ocean of love. Love is a mighty pretty thing; but like all other delicious things, it is cloying… too dainty a food to live upon *alone*." Years later, Eliza's marriage ended in scandal when she left her husband and took up with a young soldier.

opposition. He allowed Alexander Hamilton to manipulate him. France did not invade the United States, of course. Peace broke out, and Washington resigned his last commission in 1799. This time he did not bother with a farewell address.

When Connecticut governor Jonathan Trumbull, Jr., urged Washington to come out of retirement again, the old man's furious refusal revealed his utter disillusionment with the state of American political affairs. He believed the country far gone in iniquity. Federalists were arrayed against Republicans in a partisan battle that assured that faction alone commanded men's loyalties. Trumbull had begged Washington to consider standing in candidacy for a third presidential term in 1800. Though he supported the Federalists as vehemently as he condemned the Republicans—he called them the "disorganizing Party"—Washington believed that a return to the fray would be as futile as it would be personally abhorrent. No Republican would vote for him, he wrote: "Let that party set up a broomstick and call it a true son of Liberty; a Democrat, or give it any other epithet that will suit their purpose, and it will command their votes in toto!" Washington was "thoroughly convinced I should not draw a *single* vote from the Anti-federal side." The ongoing partisan conflict was the definitive repudiation of Washington's ideal of a republican nation governed by a concurring body of elite statesmen.

In July 1799, Washington wrote a will. He provided for his wife, freed his slaves, left bequests to several educational institutions, and divided his remaining estate among a host of nieces, nephews, and Custis relations. In an appendix to the will, Washington inventoried his holdings and calculated his net worth at $530,000, a figure that may have entitled him to first rank among the richest men in America.

The most important provision of the thirty-page document was the emancipation his one hundred twenty-five slaves. (More than three hundred slaves lived at Mount Vernon in 1799, but most were the property of the Custis estate; Washington had no

Parties was not so clearly drawn, and the
views of the Opposition, so clearly developed
as they are at present, — of course, allowing
your observation (as it respects myself) to
be founded, personal influence would be
of no avail. —

Let that party set up a broomstick,
and call it a true son of Liberty, — a Democrat, — or give it any other epithet that will
suit their purpose, and it will command
their votes in toto!* Will not the Federalists meet, or rather defend their cause,
on the opposite ground? — Surely they must,
or they will discover a want of Policy, in-
dicative of weakness, & pregnant of mis
chief, which cannot be admitted. — Wherein
then would lye the difference between the
present Gentlemen in Office, & myself? —

It would be matter of sore regret
to me, if I could believe that a serious tho't.
was turned towards me as his successor;
not only as it respects my ardent wishes
to pass through the vale of life in retirem't,
undisturbed in the remnant of the days I

* As an analysis of this position, look to the pend
ing Election of Governor, in Pennsylvania. —

George Washington, autograph letter to Jonathan Trumbull, July 21, 1799.

(The Gilder Lehrman Collection, on deposit at the Pierpont Morgan Library: GLC5787)

Federalist Jonathan Trumbull wanted Washington to seek a third presidential term in 1800. Only Washington's candidacy, Trumbull argued, could prevent the election of Republican Thomas Jefferson. But party loyalties now dominated American political affairs. The disillusioned Washington was sure that no Republican would vote against Jefferson: "Let that party set up a broomstick and call it a true son of Liberty; a Democrat, or give it any other epithet that will suit their purpose, and it will command their votes in toto!"

George Washington, autograph map, September 20, 1799.

(Huntington Library: HM 5994)

This "Plan of Part of the Mount Vernon Lands" that Washington drafted three months before his death laid out an elaborate crop rotation system he hoped would improve the fertility of the fields.

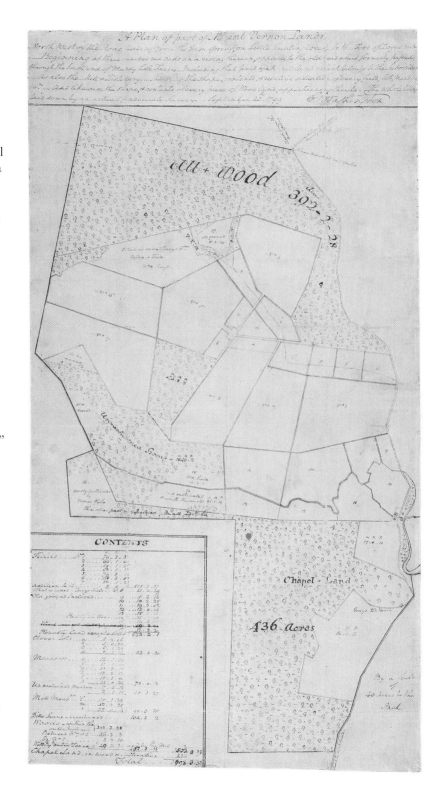

power to free them.) Washington's instructions for the future of his bondspeople appeared as the will's second clause, preceded only by the directive that his debts be paid:

> It is my Will and desire that all the Slaves which I hold in *my own right*, shall receive their freedom.... And whereas among those who will receive freedom according to this devise, there may be some, who from old age or bodily infirmities, and others who on account of their infancy, that will be unable to support themselves; it is my Will and desire that all who come under the first and second description shall be comfortably cloathed and fed by my heirs while they live; and that such of the latter description as have no parents living, or if living are unable, or unwilling to provide for them, shall be bound by the Court until they shall arrive at the age of twenty five years.... The Negros thus bound, are (by their Masters or Mistresses) to be taught to read and write; and to be brought up to some useful occupation, agreeably to the Laws of the Commonwealth of Virginia, providing for the support of Orphan and other poor Children.

The laws that Washington cited had of course been enacted for the benefit of Virginia's *white* children. His wish that the underage slaves be so educated was a bold statement of his belief in the natural abilities of the enslaved. Washington's perception of the degrading effects of slavery were hardly new. On the eve of the Revolution he had predicted that, if Americans did not resist British oppression, "custom and use, will make us as tame, & abject Slaves, as the Blacks we Rule over with such an arbitrary Sway." The warning implied that Washington believed that it was the conditions of slavery, and not any natural inferiority, that had reduced the blacks to a state of dependency. If this is an accurate reconstruction of his views, Washington was more enlightened than most other southern slaveholders. Thomas Jefferson had written that blacks were born inferior to whites in mind and body and that they could never live in American society as free people. Emancipation, Jefferson maintained, must be accompanied by a program of "colonization," the mass deportation of American blacks to an overseas colony. George Washington's visions were more expansive. The old man had come a long way from the callow planter who once sold off a rebellious slave to the West Indies for a cargo of limes and molasses.

Washington left no doubt about the importance that he attached to the provision for emancipation. Nor did he fail to recognize that it might go against the instincts of his survivors. "And I do moreover most pointedly, and most solemnly enjoin it upon my Executors," he continued, "to see that *this* clause respecting Slaves, and every part thereof be religiously fulfilled at the Epoch at which it is directed to take place; without evasion, neglect, or delay." The "Estate of George Washington, Deceased" would pay annual pensions to some of the freed people until 1833. Washington was the only one of the principal slaveholding founders to embrace emancipation. (Unfortunately, Virginia's restrictive "black laws" prevented the freed children from being taught to read and write.)

On December 12, 1799, Washington rode out in a winter storm for his customary inspection of the Mount Vernon farms. He was gone five hours. When he returned, his secretary remembered that he "appeared to be wet and the snow was hanging upon his hair." The next day Washington complained of a sore throat. He woke in real distress in the middle of the night. His throat was so swollen that he could scarcely breathe. The doctors were sent for. The sick man patiently endured the ministrations of three physicians, who bled him copiously. But Washington was already resigned to death. "I find I am going," he rasped. "My breath cannot last long; I believed from the first that the disorder would prove fatal." He said that he was about to make good on the "debt which must all pay" and that "he looked to the event with perfect resignation." George Washington was taking his own pulse when he died at about half-past ten the night of December 14.

Washington was sealed in a leaden coffin and quietly entombed in the family vault at Mount Vernon, but news of his death united Americans in an outcry of heartfelt grief. Devotion to the

HIGH STREET, From the Country Market-place PHILADELPHIA:

,with the procession in commemoration of the Death of GENERAL GEORGE WASHINGTON, December 26th 1799.

William Birch, "Procession in commemoration of the Death of General George Washington, December 26th: 1799," in *The City of Philadelphia,* **Philadelphia, 1800.**

(Huntington Library: 305000, plate 11)

Washington died at Mount Vernon on the night of December 14, 1799. Grieving Philadelphians staged this mock funeral twelve days after the great man's death.

Gold funeral medal by Joseph Perkins.

(National Museum of American History, Smithsonian Institution: 44164; 10384)

The enterprising Joseph Perkins offered his medals for sale in New England within three weeks of Washington's death. The gold medallion on the obverse is stamped with a profile of Washington within a legend reading "He in Glory, the World in Tears. GW OB D.14 99."

Gold mourning ring containing 1798 Charles-Balthazar-Julien-Févret de Saint-Mémin portrait of George Washington.

(National Museum of American History, Smithsonian Institution: 233157.01)

"IN MEMORY OF A FRIEND." Family and close friends wore mourning rings to commemorate a recent death. In his will George Washington left a bequest to each of his sisters-in-law for the purchase of "a mourning Ring of the value of one hundred dollars." The French artist Saint-Mémin had used a tracing machine to draw the profile on which this portrait is based.

memory of their hero would unite Americans for years to come. Washington's legacy proved nearly as precious to his country as had his leadership.

In 1799 the federal government had been in existence for just a decade. The Constitution had been signed twelve years before, and American independence, declared twenty-three years earlier, had been confirmed by treaty only sixteen years ago. Yet what had taken place in America since 1776 had changed history. For the United States was new also in its principles. First among those principles was the revolutionary belief that all people were created equal, and its corollary that governing power must derive from the people. The Americans had waged an ideological revolution—theirs was the first nation deliberately founded on ideas. Although Europe's powerful disdained the upstart republic, this leap of political faith had started monarchy and aristocracy on a course to oblivion.

Their brief, singular history had left Americans rather lacking in those attributes that traditionally serve to define nationhood. The country had recently been thirteen separate colonies. Americans descended from no ancestral tribe. They lacked a common religion and even, despite the dominance of English culture, a common language. George Washington remained the earliest

Mount Vernon, *Virginia, the Seat of the late* Genl. G. Washington.

Drawn Engraved & Publifhed by W. Birch Springland near Briftol Pennsylv.ª

William Birch, "Mount Vernon, Virginia, the Seat of the late Genl. G. Washington," in *The Country Seats of the United States in North America, with Some Scenes Connected with Them*, Springland, Pa., 1808.

(Huntington Library: 316042) Although Congress wanted Washington buried in a crypt beneath the Rotunda of the Capitol, his survivors placed his body in the old family tomb at Mount Vernon.

and most powerful symbol of the American nation. He had been there from the start, and from the moment he took command of the Continental Army in 1775, George Washington was the vessel of America's hope and pride. The same projection would have attended the appointment of another man, but the lofty, impassive Virginian seemed perfectly suited to assume such symbolic stature. His conscious blending of his own ambitions with the future of the United States only became stronger as the struggle of nation-building continued.

If death tended to cast Washington in a godlike light, it also worked to further remove the remote hero from the living. George Washington remains remarkable for both his presence and absence in American memory. He is at once familiar and enigmatic, as conspicuous and yet as featureless as the sheer stone obelisk raised to his memory above a city he never saw.

"Parson" Mason Locke Weems, best-selling author of one of the first of the growing legion of Washington biographies, invented such immortal legends as that of the contest between little George's

Mason Locke Weems,
The Life and Memorable Actions of George Washington...,
Philadelphia, 1800.

(Huntington Library: 75093)

"Parson" Weems's enormously popular biographies shaped American folklore. Best known of the fables Weems invented is the story of little George and his father's cherry tree.

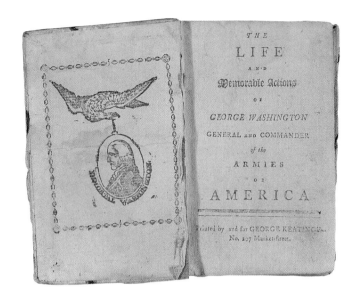

hatchet and his father's prized cherry tree. Weems fabricated his pious fables in part to instill virtue in his youthful readers. But he also hoped to cast a glow of humanity across his subject's cold marble face. Weems and his imitators wanted to make Washington a real person. They succeeded in making him ridiculous and boring. Other preposterous stories—like the celebrated wooden teeth—have gained greater hold on the national imagination than has the remarkable epic of Washington's role in the creation of the nation that he, more than any other figure, brought into being.

Like Weems, most of those who have wrestled with the colossus over the past two centuries have hoped to reveal the living Washington behind the mythological edifice. None has really succeeded. George Washington will continue to elude us. His greatness is to be found in his achievements, and those achievements are authentically monumental. So the man must remain a monument. Of the countless memorials that Washington's death called forth, however, there may be a few passages that hint at the grandeur of his legacy. In a eulogy in Congress, Fisher Ames quietly suggested that George Washington had "changed mankind's ideas of political greatness." More quietly still, Abigail Adams said, "Simple Truth is his best his Greatest Eulogy. She alone can render his Fame immortal."

Nameplate from one of Washington's military chests, Boston, 1776.

(Mount Vernon Ladies' Association)

The new commander in chief bought several second-hand trunks in Boston and attached copper nameplates engraved "Genl: Washington" to hide the initials of the former owner.

Exhibition Checklist

—◆●◆—

"Virginia Discovered and Discribed by Captain John Smith," in John Smith, *A Map of Virginia*, Oxford, 1612. (Huntington Library: 19883; Pierpont Morgan Library: PML 15911) Huntington Library copy exhibited in Los Angeles; Morgan Library copy exhibited in New York City.

George Washington, autograph manuscript ("In the year 1657, or thereabouts") May 2, 1792. (Huntington Library: HM 913)

Joseph Addison, *Cato: A tragedy*...London, 1713. (Huntington Library: 149934; Pierpont Morgan Library: PML 15587) Huntington Library copy exhibited in Los Angeles; Morgan Library copy exhibited in New York City.

Youths Behaviour, or Decency in Conversation...London, 1651. (Huntington Library: 447526)

Stem from a calumet shared by Washington and an Indian chief during his first western journey, 1748. (National Museum of American History, Smithsonian Institution: 67435, 31822)

George Washington, autograph surveys with maps, November 2, 1749; November 8, 1749; November 9, 1749; and November 10, 1749. (Pierpont Morgan Library: MA 3461. Gift of the estate of Hall Park McCullough, 1971.)

A Map of the Inhabited part of Virginia...Drawn by Joshua Fry & Peter Jefferson in 1751. London, 1755. (Huntington Library: 480575)

George Washington, *The Journal of Major George Washington, Sent...to the Commandant of the French Forces on the Ohio*...Williamsburg, 1754. (Huntington Library: 18718)

"Map of the Western parts of the Colony of Virginia, as far as the Mississipi," in George Washington, *The Journal of Major George Washington*...London, 1754. (The Gilder Lehrman Collection, on deposit at the Pierpont Pierpont Morgan Library: GLC 419.02)

[General Edward Braddock's copy], "New Works at Fort du Quesne at junction of Alligheny & Monougahila rivers," manuscript map, 1755. (Huntington Library: HM 898)

Samuel Davies, *Religion and patriotism...A sermon preached to Captain Overton's Independent company of volunteers, raised in Hanover County, Virginia, August 17, 1755.* Philadelphia, 1755. (Huntington Library: 106787; Pierpont Morgan Library: PML 3520) Huntington Library copy exhibited in Los Angeles; Morgan Library copy (London, 1756) exhibited in New York City.

George Washington, letter signed to the Earl of Loudoun, July 25, 1756. (Huntington Library: LO 1354)

George II, *Orders for Settling the Rank of the Officers of HM's Forces, When Serving with the Provincial Forces in North America.* London, 1754. (Huntington Library: 71480)

George Washington, autograph letter to the Earl of Loudoun, January 10, 1757. (Huntington Library: LO 2659)

George Washington, autograph diagram ("Plan of a line of March"), October 8, 1758. (Pierpont Morgan Library: MA 878. Purchased by Pierpont Morgan, 1908.)

George Washington, autograph document ("Invoice of sundries to be shipd by Robert Cary and Company"), September 20, 1759. (Huntington Library: HM 5244)

George Washington, autograph manuscript (diary leaf), April 1766. (Huntington Library: HM 52708)

["Plan and section of a slave-ship," 1789], in Thomas Clarkson, *The History of the Rise, Progress, and Accomplishment of the Abolition of the African Slave Trade by the British Parliament.* London, 1808. (Huntington Library: 297309)

Robert Dinwiddie, *A Proclamation...February 19, 1754,* Williamsburg, 1754. (Huntington Library: 19867)

George Washington, autograph document ("Plan of the tenements on the south Fork of Bulls Run"), [c. 1771]. (Huntington Library: HM 5508)

George Washington, autograph letter to Jonathan Boucher, May 5, 1772. (Huntington Library: HM 5274)

Silver-handled knife. (National Museum of American History, Smithsonian Institution: 13152)

Silver-handled fork. (National Museum of American History, Smithsonian Institution: 13152; 1198)

Blue and white Chinese export platter. (National Museum of American History, Smithsonian Institution: 13152; 1177)

Amber necklace worn by Martha Washington. (National Museum of American History, Smithsonian Institution: 319870.1)

Gold snuff box with Custis crest. (Mount Vernon Ladies' Association: W-2810)

Two silver teaspoons with Custis crest. (Mount Vernon Ladies' Association: W-2537)

Two silver teaspoons with Washington crest. (Mount Vernon Ladies' Association: WW-2535 A and B)

Center section of seven-piece table plateaux, c. 1770. (Mount Vernon Ladies' Association: W-2179)

[George Washington's copy, with his signature], *Instructions for Officers detached in the Field: Containing a Scheme for Forming a Partisan.* London, 1770. (Pierpont Morgan Library: PML 55169. Gift of Walter H. Page, 1965)

Paul Revere, *The Bloody Massacre perpetrated in…Boston on March 5th 1770…* Boston, 1770. (The Gilder Lehrman Collection, on deposit at the Pierpont Morgan Library: GLC 1868)

[Attributed to Philip Dawe], *The Bostonians Paying the Excise-Man or Tarring & Feathering,* London, 1774. (The Gilder Lehrman Collection, on deposit at the Pierpont Morgan Library: GLC 4961.01)

"Assemblée Du Congrès," in M. Hilliard D'Auberteuil, *Essais Historiques et Politiques sur les Anglo-Americans.* Brussels, 1781. (Huntington Library: 140869)

A Plan of the Town and Harbour of Boston and the Country adjacent with the Road from Boston to Concord Shewing the Place of the late Engagement between the King's Troops & the Provincials… J. DeCosta, London, July 29, 1775. (Huntington Library: Museum Map Store Collection, 93/578)

Pewter camp plate. (Mount Vernon Ladies' Association)

Continental Congress, manuscript document ("To George Washington, Esq.") signed twice by John Hancock, June 22, 1775. (Huntington Library: HM 22011)

Martha Washington, autograph letter to Elizabeth Ramsey, December 30, 1775. (Pierpont Morgan Library: MA 1008)

Nameplate from one of Washington's military chests, Boston, 1776. (Mount Vernon Ladies' Association)

George Washington, letter signed to Thomas Mumford, February 13, 1776. (The Gilder Lehrman Collection, on deposit at the Pierpont Morgan Library: GLC 1117)

"The Town of Falmouth, Burnt by Captain Moet, Octbr. 18th 1775," in *Impartial History of the War in America*, Boston, 1782. (Huntington Library: 180000)

Thomas Paine, *Common Sense*...Philadelphia, 1776. (Huntington Library: 92574; Pierpont Morgan Library: PML 3627. Purchased by Pierpont Morgan with the Irwin collection, 1900.) Huntington Library copy exhibited in Los Angeles; Morgan Library copy exhibited in New York City.

In Congress, July 4, 1776. A Declaration by the Representatives of the United States of America...Philadelphia: John Dunlap, 1776. (Pierpont Morgan Library: PML 77158. Gift of The Robert Wood Johnson, Jr., Charitable Trust, 1982.)

A Sketch of the Operations of His Majesty's Fleet and Army...in 1776. London, J. F. W. Des Barres, January 17, 1777. (Huntington Library: Museum Map Store Collection, 93/111)

George Washington, letter signed to James Clinton, June 29 (with post-script dated July 1), 1776. (Pierpont Morgan Library: MA 507 [2]. Purchased by Pierpont Morgan, 1906.)

Martha Washington, autograph letter to Anna Maria Dandridge Bassett, August 28, 1776. (Pierpont Morgan Library: MA 1014. Purchased in 1924.)

Ambrose Serle, manuscript journal, May 1776–July 1778, entry for July 15, 1776. (Huntington Library: HM 583)

François X. Habermann, *Representation du Feu terrible a Nouvelle Yorck...19 Septembre 1776*, Augsburg, [c. 1777]. (Huntington Library: 88539)

François X. Habermann, *L'Entré triumphale de Troops royales a Nouvelle Yorck*...Augsburg, [c. 1777.] The Gilder Lehrman Collection, on deposit at the Pierpont Morgan Library: GLC 5860)

After Charles Willson Peale, "George Washington at the battle of Princeton," 1779. (Huntington Art Collections: 19:13)

Two stars from General Washington's uniform, with locks of hair of

George and Martha Washington. (Pierpont Morgan Library: MA 6029. Gift of Louisa Lee Schuyler and Georgina Schuyler, 1924.)

Flintlock horse pistol with "G. W." monogram, one of a pair owned by George Washington, London. (Mount Vernon Ladies' Association: W-480/B)

[William White], *The horse America throwing his master*, London, 1779. (Huntington Library: cartoon collection)

Benjamin Huntington, autograph manuscript, April 30, 1781. (The Gilder Lehrman Collection, on deposit at the Pierpont Morgan Library: GLC 318)

George Washington, autograph letter to John Laurens, January 30, 1781. (Huntington Library: HM 5391)

Pierre Joseph Jeunot, [battle of the Chesapeake Capes, September 5, 1781]. (Huntington Library: HM 578)

Charles, Earl Cornwallis, letter to George Washington, October 17, 1781. (Pierpont Morgan Library: MA 488. Purchased by Pierpont Morgan, 1908.)

Alexander Ross, "The Garrisons of York & Gloucester including the Officers & Seamen of His Britannick Majesty's Ships as well as other Mariners to surrender themselves Prisoners of War to the Combined Forces of America & France," manuscript document, [October 18, 1781]. (Pierpont Morgan Library: MA 488 [11]. Purchased by Pierpont Morgan, 1906.)

George Washington, autograph letter to James McHenry, October 17, 1782. (Huntington Library: MH 128)

George III, autograph letter to Thomas Townshend, November 19, 1782. (Huntington Library: HM 25755)

Thomas Townshend, autograph manuscript, September 19, 1782. (Huntington Library: HM 25758)

George Washington, autograph letter signed to Tench Tilghman, January 10, 1783. (Huntington Library: HM 5441)

George Washington, autograph letter to Joseph Jones, March 12, 1783. (Huntington Library: HM 5262)

George Washington, manuscript address ("To the Genls., Fields, & Other Officers Assembled"), March [15,] 1783. (Huntington Library: HM 1607)

George Washington, letter signed (the "Circular Letter to the States") to George Clinton, June 21, 1783. (Pierpont Morgan Library: MA 507)

"Mrs: General Washington Bestowing thirteen Stripes on Britannia," in *The Rambler's Magazine...for March 1783*. London, 1783. (Huntington Library: 478018)

George Washington, autograph document ("The United States in Account with G. Washington"), December 13–28, 1783. (Huntington Library: HM 5502)

Jean-Antoine Houdon, "George Washington," plaster bust, 1787. (Dr. Gary Milan)

George Washington, autograph letter to Henry Knox, February 20, 1784. (The Gilder Lehrman Collection, on deposit at the Pierpont Morgan Library: 2437 LIII, 59)

"Plan of an American New Cleared Farm," in Patrick Campbell, *Travels in....North America in the Years 1791 and 1792*, Edinburgh, 1793. (Huntington Library: 18609)

"General Washington's Jack Ass," in *Weatherwise's Town and Country Almanack for...1786*. Boston, [1785]. (Huntington Library: 424665)

[George Washington's copy], *Descriptions of some of the Utensils in Husbandry, Rolling Carriages, Cart Rollers, and Divided Rollers for Land or Gardens, Mills, Weighing Engines, &c. &C. Made and Sold by James Sharp*. London, [c. 1785]. (Pierpont Morgan Library: unaccessioned books)

George Washington, autograph letter to John Francis Mercer, September 9, 1786. (The Gilder Lehrman Collection, on deposit at the Pierpont Morgan Library: GLC 3705)

George Washington, autograph letter to James McHenry, November 11, 1786. (The Gilder Lehrman Collection, on deposit at the Pierpont Morgan Library: GLC 2065)

George Washington, autograph map of Mount Vernon, December 1799. (Huntington Library: HM 5995)

George Washington, autograph letter to Tobias Lear, May 6, 1794. (Huntington Library: HM 5229)

George Washington, autograph letter to James McHenry, August 22, 1785. (Huntington Library: HM 5475)

George Washington, autograph letter to Benjamin Lincoln, November

7, 1786. (The Gilder Lehrman Collection, on deposit at the Pierpont Morgan Library: GLC 1479)

George Washington, autograph letter to Henry Knox, February 3, 1787. (The Gilder Lehrman Collection, on deposit at the Pierpont Morgan Library: GLC 2437 LIII, 65)

George Washington, autograph letter to Henry Knox, February 25, 1787. (The Gilder Lehrman Collection, on deposit at the Pierpont Morgan Library: GLC 2437 LIII, 66)

Cincinnati platter. (The Louise and Barry Taper Collection)

Custine cup and saucer with GW cipher. (The Louise and Barry Taper Collection)

Sèvres plate. (Mount Vernon Ladies' Association: W-612)

Sèvres porringer. (Mount Vernon Ladies' Association: W-1457)

Pierce Butler, autograph manuscript ("Resolved therefore that a National Government ought to be Established"), May 30, 1787. (The Gilder Lehrman Collection, on deposit at the Pierpont Morgan Library: GLC 819.04)

Pierce Butler, autograph manuscript (draft of the fugitive slave cause), [c. August 28, 1787]. (The Gilder Lehrman Collection, on deposit at the Pierpont Morgan Library: GLC 819.17)

Pierce Butler, autograph manuscript ("Resolved that it is the opinion of this Convention that the Teritory of the States is too extensive to Consist of One Republic only"), [c. August 1787]. (The Gilder Lehrman Collection, on deposit at the Pierpont Morgan Library: GLC 819.23)

We the People of the States of New-Hampshire, Massachusetts, Rhode-Island, [Report of the Committee of Detail], Philadelphia, August 6, 1787. (The Gilder Lehrman Collection, on deposit at the Pierpont Morgan Library: GLC 819.01; Pierpont Morgan Library: PML 16504. Purchased by Pierpont Morgan, 1907.) Gilder Lehrman Collection copy exhibited in Los Angeles; Morgan Library copy exhibited in New York City.

We the People of the United States, [United States Constitution, the "Members' edition," inscribed by Benjamin Franklin], Philadelphia, 1787. (The Gilder Lehrman Collection, on deposit at the Pierpont Morgan Library: GLC 3585)

Charles Willson Peale, "A N.W. View of the State House in

Philadelphia taken in 1778," in *Columbian Magazine*, Philadelphia, July 1787. (Huntington Library: 39002)

George Washington, autograph letter to Henry Knox, August 19, 1787. (The Gilder Lehrman Collection, on deposit at the Pierpont Morgan Library: GLC 2437 LIII, 69)

[George Washington's set, with his signatures], Adam Ferguson, *The History of the Progress and Termination of the Roman Republic.* 3 vols., London, 1788. (Pierpont Morgan Library: PML 5390–5392. Acquired by Pierpont Morgan before 1913.)

George Washington, autograph letter to Richard Conway, March 4, 1789. (Pierpont Morgan Library: MA 878. Purchased by Pierpont Morgan, 1908.)

George Washington, autograph letter to Henry Knox, April 1, 1789. (The Gilder Lehrman Collection, on deposit at the Pierpont Morgan Library: GLC 2437 LIII, 74)

"View of Federal Hall, New York," in *The Massachusetts Magazine*, Boston, May 1789. (Huntington Library: 251823)

"Plan of the City of New York," in *New-York Directory…for 1789*. New York, 1789. (Huntington Library: 15038)

Commemorative clothing button from Washington's inauguration, 1789. (National Museum of American History, Smithsonian Institution: 227739.1789.B1)

Commemorative clothing button from Washington's inauguration, 1789. (National Museum of American History, Smithsonian Institution: 1980.0771.02)

George Washington, autograph letter to James Madison, August 5, 1789. (Huntington Library: HM 5100)

Order of Procession, to be Observed on the Arrival of the President…Providence, August 17, 1790. Providence, 1790. (Huntington Library: 108388)

Silver-plated Argand table lamp, c. 1790. (Mount Vernon Ladies' Association: W-1871)

George Washington, autograph letter to Tobias Lear, October 14, 1791. (Huntington Library: HM 5220)

Alexander Hamilton, *Report…to the House of Representatives…for the Support of the public credit of the United States*. New York, 1790. (Huntington Library: 24924; The Gilder Lehrman Collection, on deposit at the

Pierpont Morgan Library: GLC 960) Huntington Library copy exhibited in Los Angeles; Gilder Lehrman Collection copy exhibited in New York City.

William Birch, "Bank of the United States," in *The City of Philadelphia*, Philadelphia, 1800. (Huntington Library: 305000, plate 17)

George Washington, document signed (proclamation concerning the Eels River or Miami Indians), May 7, 1793. (Huntington Library: HM 5550)

George Washington, letter signed to the Soldier, Chiefs and Warriors, May 7, 1793. (Huntington Library: HM 3988)

William Birch, "Back of the State House," in *The City of Philadelphia*, Philadelphia, 1800. (Huntington Library: 305000, plate 22)

[Andrew Ellicot], *Plan of the city of Washington...Seat of Government after the Year [1800]*, Philadelphia, 1792. (Huntington Library: 443542)

[Attributed to Nicholas King, view of the President's House, Treasury Department, and Blodgett's Hotel, Washington, D.C., c. 1800–10.] Huntington Library: HM 52665)

George Washington, autograph letter to James Madison, May 20, 1792. (Pierpont Morgan Library: MA 505. Purchased by Pierpont Morgan with the Ford Collection, before 1900.)

George Washington, autograph letter to Henry Lee, January 20, 1793. (The Gilder Lehrman Collection, on deposit at the Pierpont Morgan Library: GLC 2793.002)

William Birch, "Congress Hall," in *The City of Philadelphia*, Philadelphia, 1800. (Huntington Library: 305000, plate 20)

Pocket watch, English, 1793–94. (Mount Vernon Ladies' Association: W-446)

Satin waistcoat. (Mount Vernon Ladies' Association: W-575)

George Washington, autograph letter to Gouverneur Morris, March 25, 1793. (The Gilder Lehrman Collection, on deposit at the Pierpont Morgan Library: GLC 494)

George Washington, manuscript annotated and signed (draft of the 1794 Annual Message), November 1794. (The Gilder Lehrman Collection, on deposit at the Pierpont Morgan Library: GLC 1054)

*Treaty of Amity, Commerce & Navigation, between his Britannic Majesty, and the United States of America...*Philadelphia, 1795. (Huntington Library:

66613; The Gilder Lehrman Collection, on deposit at the Pierpont Morgan Library: GLC3673.01) Huntington Library copy exhibited in Los Angeles; Gilder Lehrman Collection copy (London, 1795) exhibited in New York City.

Thomas Paine, *Letter to George Washington...*Philadelphia, 1796. (Huntington Library: 7802)

Mad Tom in a Rage. (Huntington Library: cartoon collection)

George Washington, *Address to the People of the United States...Expressing his determination not to be considered as a Candidate for the Presidency at the next Election,* Exeter [New Hampshire], 1796. (Huntington Library: 72886); ["The Farewell Address" with Washington's autograph notes] in Claypoole's *Daily American Advertiser,* Philadelphia, September 19, 1796. (The Gilder Lehrman Collection, on deposit at the Pierpont Morgan Library: GLC 185) Huntington Library copy exhibited in Los Angeles; Gilder Lehrman Collection copy exhibited in New York City.

Gilbert Stuart, "George Washington," 1797. (The Virginia Steele Scott Collection, Huntington Art Collections: 39.1. Gift of Mrs. Alexander Baring, 1939.)

Chinese export porcelain covered cup from "a Box of china for Lady Washington." (National Museum of American History, Smithsonian Institution: 13152; 1238; and 1240)

George Washington, autograph letter to Henry Knox, March 2, 1797. (The Gilder Lehrman Collection, on deposit at the Pierpont Morgan Library: GLC 2437 LIII, 86)

Sheraton-style side chair. (National Museum of American History, Smithsonian Institution: 13152)

Silver candlestick. (National Museum of American History, Smithsonian Institution: 13152; 1182)

Oval silver tray. (National Museum of American History, Smithsonian Institution: 13152; 1189)

Silver bottle stand. (National Museum of American History, Smithsonian Institution: 13152; 1187)

George Washington, autograph letter to Sir Isaac Heard, May 2, 1792. (Huntington Library: HM 913)

George Washington, autograph letter to Eliza Parke Custis, September 14, 1794. (Pierpont Morgan Library: MA 503. Purchased by Pierpont Morgan with the Ford Collection, before 1900.)

George Washington, autograph letter to Jonathan Trumbull, July 21, 1799. (The Gilder Lehrman Collection, on deposit at the Pierpont Morgan Library: GLC5787)

George Washington, autograph map ("A Plan of Part of the Mount Vernon Lands"), September 20, 1799. (Huntington Library: HM 5994)

George Washington, *The Last Will and Testament of…with a schedule of his property*, Philadelphia, 1800. (Huntington Library: 105259)

William Birch, "High Street, from the Country Marketplace Philadelphia: with the procession in commemoration of the Death of General George Washington, December 26th: 1799," in *The City of Philadelphia*, Philadelphia, 1800. (Huntington Library: 305000, plate 11)

Henry Lee, *A Funeral Oration, in Honour of the Memory of George Washington…* Brooklyn, 1800. (Huntington Library: 37804; Pierpont Morgan Library: PML) Huntington Library copy exhibited in Los Angeles; Morgan Library copy exhibited in New York City.

Mason Locke Weems, *The Life and Memorable Actions of George Washington…* Philadelphia, 1800. (Huntington Library: 75093)

William Birch, "Mount Vernon, Virginia, the Seat of the late Genl. G. Washington," in *The Country Seats of the United States in North America, with Some Scenes Connected with Them*. Springland, Pa., 1808. (Huntington Library: 316042)

Gold mourning ring containing 1798 Charles-Balthazar-Julien-Févret de Saint-Mémin portrait of George Washington. (National Museum of American History, Smithsonian Institution: 233157.01)

Gold funeral medal by Joseph Perkins. (National Museum of American History, Smithsonian Institution: 44164; 10384)

Elisha Cullen Dick, "George Washington," c. 1799 (after James Sharples's 1796 portrait. (Mount Vernon Ladies' Association: H-258)

William Matthew Prior, "Evening," 1850. (Mount Vernon Ladies' Association: M-3702)

Suggested Reading

————◆◆◆————

ONE-VOLUME BIOGRAPHIES

John R. Alden, *George Washington: A Biography* (Baton Rouge: Louisiana State University Press, 1984).

Marcus Cunliffe, *George Washington: Man and Monument* (Boston: Little, Brown, 1954).

John E. Ferling, *The First of Men: A Life of George Washington* (Knoxville: University of Tennessee Press, 1988).

Robert F. Jones, *George Washington* (rev. ed., New York: Fordham University Press, 1986).

MULTIPLE-VOLUME BIOGRAPHIES

James Thomas Flexner, *George Washington*, 4 vols. (Boston: Little, Brown, 1965–72; 1-vol. abridgement, 1974).

Douglas Southall Freeman, *George Washington*, 7 vols. (New York: Charles Scribner's Sons, 1949–1957; vol. 7 completed by John A. Carroll and Mary Wells Ashworth; 1-vol. abridgement by Richard Harwell, 1968).

SPECIAL STUDIES

Richard Brookhiser, *Founding Father: Rediscovering George Washington* (New York: Free Press, 1996).

Don Higginbotham, *George Washington and the American Military Tradition* (Athens: University of Georgia Press, 1985).

Richard M. Ketchum, *The World of George Washington* (New York: American Heritage, 1974).

Paul K. Longmore, *The Invention of George Washington* (Berkeley: University of California Press, 1988).

Edmund S. Morgan, *The Genius of George Washington* (New York: W. W. Norton, 1980).

Barry Schwartz, *George Washington: The Making of an American Symbol* (New York: Free Press, 1987).

Garry Wills, *Cincinnatus: George Washington and the Enlightenment* (New York: Doubleday, 1984).

WASHINGTON'S WRITINGS

The Writings of George Washington from the Original Manuscript Sources, 1745 –1799, edited by John C. Fitzpatrick (39 vols., Washington, D.C.: U.S. Government Printing Office, 1931 –44). The most comprehensive edition to date contains some 17,000 documents written by Washington.

The Papers of George Washington, founded at the University of Virginia in 1968, has published nearly 40 of a projected 90 volumes edited by Donald Jackson, W. W. Abbot, Dorothy Twohig, Philander D. Chase, and others (Charlottesville: University Press of Virginia). Publication of *The Papers of George Washington* goes forward in several chronological series: *Diaries; Colonial Series; Revolutionary War Series; Confederation Series; Presidential Series;* and *Retirement Series.* When complete, this edition will provide texts of more than 100,000 documents written by or addressed to Washington.

George Washington, Writings, edited by John Rhodehamel (New York: Library of America, 1997). Single-volume collection containing 450 documents.

Index